Betty Crocker

quick

30 minutes or less to dinner

&easy

Houghton Mifflin Harcourt
Boston   New York

general mills

Editorial Director: Jeff Nowak

Assistant Manager, Marketing Services:
Christine Gray

Editor: Grace Wells

Food Editors: Andrea Bidwell,
Catherine Swanson

Editorial Assistant: Kelly Gross

Recipe Development and Testing:
Betty Crocker Kitchens

Photography: General Mills Photography
Studios and Image Library

Photographers: Val Bourassa,
Maja Sahlberg, Kayla Pieper

Food Stylists: Carol Grones,
Amy Peterson

Publisher: Natalie Chapman

Associate Publisher: Jessica Goodman

Executive Editor: Anne Ficklen

Editor: Adam Kowit

Senior Editorial Assistant:
Heather Dabah

Production Editor: Abby Saul

Cover Design: Suzanne Sunwoo

Art Director: Tai Blanche

Interior Design and Layout:
Holly Wittenberg

Manufacturing Manager: Kevin Watt

Published by Houghton Mifflin Harcourt Publishing Company

Published simultaneously in Canada

For information about permission to reproduce
selections from this book, write to trade.Permissions@hmhco.com or to Permissions,
Houghton Mifflin Harcourt Publishing Company,
3 Park Avenue, 19th Floor New York, New York 10016

www.hmhco.com

Library of Congress Cataloging-in-Publication Data is available upon request.

ISBN: 978-1-118-23069-5 (pbk.); 978-1-118-28847-4 (ebk.); 978-1-118-28864-1
(ebk.); 978-1-118-28869-6 (ebk.)

Manufactured in China
SCP 10 9 8 7
4500800544

Cover photos: (clockwise) Honey-Dijon Turkey Tenderloins with Fresh
Asparagus (page 98), Tortilla Green Chili (page 261), Spicy Oven-Fried Chicken
Tenders with Gorgonzola Dip (page 50), Cranberry-Pistachio Brussels Sprouts
(page 278)

**The Betty Crocker Kitchens seal guarantees
success in your kitchen. Every recipe has
been tested in America's Most Trusted
Kitchens™ to meet our high standards of
reliability, easy preparation and great taste.**

FIND MORE GREAT IDEAS AT
BettyCrocker.com

dear friends,

It's that time of day again—and what's for dinner? It does seem like a never-ending task to get a meal on the table quickly—and have everyone love it. But with this beautiful book of 150 quick and easy recipes at your fingertips, you'll have everything you need for a great-tasting speedy supper. Each recipe is quicker to get ready than picking up takeout, and a home-cooked meal is so much better!

Pressed for time? Every recipe in the book can be on your table in 30 minutes or less and comes with a mouthwatering color photo. Plus, easy menu tips on many of the recipes give you a start on "go-with" side ideas to make meals complete. You'll be delighted with recipes like Toasted Pesto–Chicken Sausage Sandwiches (page 78), Butternut Squash Risotto (page 233) and Spicy Caprese Pizza (page 246), plus many more ideas for salads, soups, sandwiches and skillet dishes and a nice selection of grilled ideas.

And don't miss the "mini" recipes on the first page of each chapter giving you fresh ideas for really quick meals. You'll love the Fast Veggie Sides (page 268), and the Burger Bash Ideas (page 120) is just what the cook ordered! Look for Deliciously Easy Salad Combos, too (page 324)—they're perfect when you want something tasty to pair with a main dish.

So don't go for takeout; plan to eat in. With these great recipes and tips, you'll be a pro at making delicious dinners in no time.

it's quick and easy—happy cooking!

Betty Crocker

contents

quick cooking tips

With our busy schedules, we are all on the lookout for ideas to make meals easier and faster to put together. Here are some tips to help you start putting dinner on the table in record time.

- **Shop smart:** Keep a running list of items that you run out of—and group similarities together. For instance, list all of the dairy together, the veggies and fruits together, etc. You'll save time when shopping and have less of a chance to forget something.

- **Think ahead:** Instead of that last-minute dinner dash to the grocery store, plan ahead to have ingredients on hand for your favorite recipes. Then you'll be on the fast track to get dinner on the table quickly when you arrive home.

- **Get ingredients ready ahead of time:** There's no rule that says you can't chop twice the onion or bell pepper when you have the cutting board out. Just wrap the extra in a plastic bag and refrigerate or freeze for another meal. Stretch this idea to other foods—make burger patties or cook extra chicken and freeze, brown ground beef for future meals, etc.

- **Organize the kitchen for convenience:** Store items where they are convenient for cooking. Products that you might use while cooking should be close to the cooking area. Group foods that are similar together—such as all of the dry pasta in one place, spices and herbs together, canned foods readily accessible in one place and baking products such as flour and sugar together.

- **Keep order in the freezer:** It's easy to forget foods that get pushed to the back. Store packages of vegetables separate from meats and try to stack items so that they are easy to see. Label anything that you add to the freezer and include a date.

- **Prioritize the foods in the refrigerator:** Keep fresh veggies and fruits separate from the meat and cheeses. Place condiments all in one area of the refrigerator. Keep track of what needs to be used up first, then try to incorporate these items in meals.

- **Clean up as you work:** While you are prepping the meal, it's easy to quickly wash a chopping board, knife and measuring utensil—leaving you with less to do after the meal. Keep counters clean too—it just makes things go faster.

gizmos and gadgets

Having the right (or convenient) tool or product when you need it can shave minutes off prep time. Look for the following items in department or grocery stores and specialty kitchen stores. Keep items that you use frequently close to the cooking area to save even more time.

Cutting boards: Have at least two boards, one for vegetables and fruits and the other for meat. Choose from several materials. Plastic and acrylic are easy to clean in the dishwasher. Wood boards do not dull knives as quickly but may not be able to go in the dishwasher.

Food processor or chopper: For small amounts, a mini processor or chopper quickly chops vegetables and other foods. Use a larger processor for bigger amounts.

Freezer containers and bags: Use these for storing prepped ingredients and leftovers.

Instant-read thermometer: With this handy tool, you can quickly check the temperature of meats or soups. It cannot be used in the oven but is a great tool to have available for quick checks.

Measuring utensils: Plan to have a variety of tools in the kitchen to make accurate measuring quick and easy. Items to include are glass or plastic measuring cups, dry measures and measuring spoons.

Nonstick foil and pan-lining paper: Lining pans with nonstick foil or coated pan-lining foil makes cleanup simply a breeze!

Sharp knives and sharpener: Choose a variety of knives for the kitchen and keep them sharp. Invest in a knife sharpener to do this—it's a great investment. Sharp knives make chopping and slicing much easier than dull ones.

Tongs: For convenience, have a couple sizes of tongs available and use them for turning, stirring and removing items from pans.

Whisk: A wire or plastic whisk is an invaluable tool—use it for sauces, dressings and just plain mixing.

dinner dash pantry

What's for dinner? Most of us start thinking about dinner about an hour or two before we actually sit down to eat. Whether you're still at work or the kids are just getting off the bus, that's not very far ahead of time. A well-stocked pantry is a solution for this last-minute scramble and is a terrific meal-planning tool. Since we all like different foods and have different needs, no one pantry list works for everyone, but these lists of quick picks for pantry items, produce, meat, dairy and seasonings provide a great starting place to build your own "dinner dash pantry." Then you can add items as you find more favorite recipes.

vegetables

- Prewashed and precut fresh vegetables
- Frozen veggies (plain or blends)
- Salad kits
- Canned veggies (mushrooms, corn)
- Ready-to-heat-and-eat refrigerated potato side dishes
- Frozen and refrigerated ready-to-cook potatoes
- Boxed instant potato mixes

fruits

- Prewashed and precut fresh fruit
- Frozen fruit
- Jarred and canned fruit

meat, poultry, fish and seafood

- Ground beef and turkey
- Precut meats and chicken
- Boneless skinless chicken breasts
- Thinly cut meats and poultry
- Steaks and chops instead of roasts
- Heat-and-eat seasoned roasts
- Rotisserie chicken
- Refrigerated shredded barbecued meat and poultry
- Deli products
- Canned and vacuum-packed pouch products
- Refrigerated seasoned meat and poultry strips
- Precooked sausage links and rings
- Frozen meatballs
- Frozen breaded chicken and fish
- Frozen peeled deveined shrimp or breaded shrimp

dairy case

- Milk
- Eggs or fat-free egg product
- Butter or margarine
- Shredded, sliced, crumbled and cubed cheeses
- Cheese spreads, cheese loaves
- Grated Parmesan cheese
- Cream cheese
- Half-and-half, whipping cream
- Sour cream

nonperishable staples

- Soups and chili
- Pasta and pizza sauces
- Jarred gravy
- Gravy and sauce mixes
- Canned seasoned tomato products
- Canned chicken and beef broth
- Canned beans (plain, refried or baked beans)
- Dried fruits
- Nuts
- Vegetable oil
- Olive oil
- Cooking spray

pastas and grains

- Fresh refrigerated pasta (plain or filled)
- Frozen egg noodles
- Frozen ravioli or gnocchi
- Angel hair or vermicelli pasta
- Couscous (plain or flavored)
- Flavored pasta and noodle mixes
- Instant white or brown rice
- Flavored rice mixes

condiments

- Salsa
- Ketchup
- Barbecue sauce
- Mustard (yellow, Dijon, honey mustard)
- Mayonnaise or salad dressing
- Soy sauce, teriyaki sauce
- Marinades
- Worcestershire sauce
- Balsamic vinegar
- Salad dressings
- Pickles/olives
- Dried herbs (basil, oregano, Italian seasoning, marjoram, thyme)
- Spices (cinnamon, ginger, cloves, pumpkin pie spice, chili powder, cumin)
- Seasonings and seasoning mixes (garlic powder and salt, lemon-pepper, Cajun, barbecue)
- Honey
- Maple syrup
- Jams, jellies, marmalades, preserves
- Jarred chopped garlic
- Refrigerated or jarred pesto
- Bouillon granules or cubes

breads and baking mixes

- Tortillas
- Prebaked Italian pizza crusts
- Taco shells
- Bread crumbs (plain or seasoned)
- Croutons
- Stuffing mix or cubes
- Frozen dinner rolls
- Refrigerated dough products (biscuits, rolls, pizza dough, piecrust)
- French bread
- Pita breads
- English muffins
- Bread (your favorite type of loaf)
- Bisquick mix (for pancakes, biscuits, dumplings)

ultra-convenience

- Frozen pizza
- Frozen meal starter kits
- Frozen seasoned pasta blends
- Boxed meal kits
- Stop by the deli
- Pick up your favorite takeout
- Order pizza
- Make reservations!

three-ingredient pasta sauces

Turn a few everyday ingredients into a great sauce for your favorite hot cooked plain or filled pasta. Top with grated, shredded or shaved Asiago or Parmesan cheese. You might also like to offer freshly ground black pepper and crushed red pepper flakes as a final garnish.

1 Artichoke, Olive and Sun-Dried Tomato Sauce: Heat 1 can (14 ounces) undrained marinated artichoke hearts, coarsely chopped, ¼ cup sliced drained sun-dried tomatoes in oil and 2 tablespoons sliced ripe olives until hot.

2 Parsley-Bacon Sauce: Heat 10 ounces (1¼ cups) refrigerated Alfredo sauce, 2 slices cooked bacon, crumbled, and ¼ cup chopped fresh parsley until hot.

3 Cheesy Cheddar and Meatball Sauce: Heat 1 jar (14 to 16 ounces) double Cheddar or roasted garlic pasta sauce, 8 ounces cooked Italian meatballs (halved or quartered if large) and 2 tablespoons chopped fresh basil until hot.

4 Margherita Pasta Sauce: Heat 1 can (14.5 ounces) undrained diced tomatoes with garlic, 2 tablespoons chopped fresh basil or oregano and ½ cup mozzarella cheese cubes until hot.

5 Shrimp Marinara Sauce: Heat 10 ounces (1¼ cups) refrigerated marinara sauce, 8 ounces cooked medium shrimp and 2 tablespoons chopped fresh basil until hot.

6 Pepperoni and Olive Sauce: Heat 1 cup tomato pasta sauce or pizza sauce, 4 ounces chopped pepperoni and 2 tablespoons sliced ripe olives until hot.

bruschetta banquet

Brush tops of 30 baguette slices (about a 1-pound loaf) with olive oil. Toast in the oven at 375°F for 8 to 10 minutes or until crisp.

1 Artichoke Bruschetta: Spread toasted baguette slices with artichoke or spinach dip. Sprinkle with shredded or shaved Asiago or Parmesan cheese. Serve as is or broil about 1 minute, until cheese is melted.

2 Beef Tenderloin Bruschetta: Spread toasted baguette slices with chive-and-onion cream cheese spread thinned with a little milk. Top with thinly sliced beef tenderloin or roast beef (from deli), thinly sliced or chopped plum (Roma) tomato and chopped fresh parsley.

3 Black Bean–Cotija Bruschetta: Spread toasted baguette slices with black bean dip or refried black beans and top with salsa. Sprinkle with crumbled cotija cheese or shredded Cheddar and whole or chopped fresh cilantro leaves.

4 BLT Bruschetta: Spread toasted baguette slices with mayonnaise or salad dressing. Top with shredded lettuce, well-drained chopped seeded tomato and crumbled cooked bacon.

5 Brie, Raspberry and Pear Bruschetta: Lightly spread toasted baguette slices with seedless raspberry preserves. Top with thinly sliced pear and thin slices of Brie cheese. Serve as is or broil about 1 minute, until cheese is melted.

6 Caramelized Onion–Gorgonzola Bruschetta: Melt 1 tablespoon butter in 10-inch skillet. Thinly slice 1 large sweet onion; cook uncovered in butter over medium-high heat 10 minutes, stirring 3 or 4 times. Sprinkle with 1/8 teaspoon salt; cook covered over medium-low heat 25 to 30 minutes, stirring every 5 minutes, until onions are deep golden brown. Top toasted baguette slices with the onions. Sprinkle with crumbled Gorgonzola cheese. Serve as is or broil about 1 minute, until cheese is melted.

7 Pesto-Mascarpone Bruschetta: Spread toasted baguette slices with mascarpone cheese or softened cream cheese. Top with basil pesto and sprinkle with chopped red bell pepper and toasted pine nuts.

8 Smoked Salmon Bruschetta: Arrange thinly sliced smoked salmon on toasted baguette slices. Top with dollop of sour cream. Sprinkle lightly with grated lemon zest and chopped fresh chives or small sprigs of fresh dill.

9 *(no photo)* **Chicken and Roasted Pepper Bruschetta:** Spread toasted baguette slices with ranch dressing. Top with shredded rotisserie chicken and sliced roasted bell peppers (from a jar). Sprinkle with chopped fresh basil.

10 *(no photo)* **Grilled Cheese Bruschetta:** Spread toasted baguette slices with Dijon mustard and top with thin slices of Cheddar cheese. Sprinkle with chopped fresh chives. Broil about 1 minute, until cheese is melted.

light bites

blt tomato cups

PREP TIME **30 MINUTES** START TO FINISH **30 MINUTES** **24 APPETIZERS**

6 slices bacon, cut into ½-inch slices

12 small plum (Roma) tomatoes

3 cups coarsely chopped romaine lettuce (6 leaves)

2 tablespoons ranch dressing

2 tablespoons coarsely crushed garlic-and-butter-flavor croutons

1 In 10-inch nonstick skillet over medium heat, cook bacon 5 to 7 minutes until crisp; drain on paper towels.

2 With serrated knife, cut each tomato in half crosswise. Using teaspoon, scoop out seeds and pulp from each tomato half, leaving enough tomato for a firm shell. If necessary, cut small slice from bottom so tomato half stands upright.

3 In medium bowl, combine lettuce and ranch dressing. Using small tongs or fingers, fill tomato shells evenly with lettuce mixture. Sprinkle with bacon and croutons. Serve immediately or refrigerate for up to 1 hour before serving.

1 APPETIZER: Calories 25; Total Fat 1.5g (Saturated Fat 0g; Trans Fat 0g); Cholesterol 0mg; Sodium 60mg; Total Carbohydrate 1g (Dietary Fiber 0g); Protein 1g **EXCHANGES:** ½ Vegetable, ½ Fat **CARBOHYDRATE CHOICES:** 0

easy add-on

If desired, sprinkle the cups evenly with about 2 tablespoons of finely shredded Cheddar cheese.

mini salmon wraps

PREP TIME **20 MINUTES**   START TO FINISH **30 MINUTES**   **48 APPETIZERS**

2 **packages (3 oz each) cream cheese, softened**

2 **tablespoons horseradish sauce**

6 **spinach, tomato or plain flour tortillas (8 to 10 inches)**

1 **medium cucumber, peeled, finely chopped (1 cup)**

¼ **cup sour cream**

¼ **cup chopped fresh dill weed**

¼ **cup finely chopped red or yellow onion**

8 **oz salmon lox, cut into thin strips**

1 In small bowl, mix cream cheese and horseradish sauce. Spread cream cheese mixture evenly over tortillas.

2 In small bowl, mix cucumber, sour cream, dill weed and onion; spread over cream cheese mixture. Arrange salmon strips over cucumber mixture. Roll up tortillas tightly.

3 Cover and refrigerate wraps 10 minutes or until ready to serve. Cut each wrap into 8 pieces.

1 APPETIZER: Calories 40; Total Fat 2g (Saturated Fat 1g; Trans Fat 0g); Cholesterol 5mg; Sodium 90mg; Total Carbohydrate 3g (Dietary Fiber 0g); Protein 1g **EXCHANGES:** ½ Fat **CARBOHYDRATE CHOICES:** 0

make it ahead

Beat the clock! Make these sophisticated wraps up to 24 hours ahead; cover with plastic wrap and refrigerate until serving time.

20 minutes or less

beef and spinach roll-ups

PREP TIME **15 MINUTES** START TO FINISH **15 MINUTES** **24 APPETIZERS**

¼ cup mayonnaise or
 salad dressing

½ teaspoon **garlic powder**

2 **spinach-flavored tortillas**
 (8 to 10 inches)

1 cup **fresh spinach**

¼ lb **thinly sliced cooked**
 roast beef

¾ cup **shredded Cheddar cheese**
 (3 oz)

1 medium **tomato, chopped**

1 In small bowl, mix mayonnaise and garlic powder. Spread mixture evenly over tortillas.

2 Top tortillas with layers of spinach, roast beef, cheese and tomato; roll up tightly. Trim ends from rolls. Cut each roll into 12 slices; secure with toothpicks. Serve immediately or refrigerate until ready to serve.

1 APPETIZER: Calories 50; Total Fat 4g (Saturated Fat 1.5g; Trans Fat 0g); Cholesterol 10mg; Sodium 60mg; Total Carbohydrate 2g (Dietary Fiber 0g); Protein 2g **EXCHANGES:** 1 Fat **CARBOHYDRATE CHOICES:** 0

instant success

Spinach leaves are sometimes sandy, so be sure to thoroughly wash them well in cool water. Dry them well with paper towels before making the roll-ups.

20 minutes or less

pimiento cheese spread appetizers

PREP TIME **15 MINUTES**   START TO FINISH **15 MINUTES**   **16 APPETIZERS**

⅔ cup small whole pimiento-stuffed green olives (from 10-oz jar)

1 cup shredded Cheddar cheese (4 oz)

¼ cup mayonnaise or salad dressing

1 package (3 oz) cream cheese, softened

Pinch ground red pepper (cayenne)

16 slices cocktail rye bread

1 Reserve 16 whole olives for garnish. Chop remaining olives; place in medium bowl. Add Cheddar cheese, mayonnaise, cream cheese and red pepper; beat with electric mixer on medium speed until well blended.

2 Spread about 2 tablespoons cheese mixture on 8 of the bread slices. Top with remaining bread slices. Cut each sandwich diagonally in half.

3 Garnish each appetizer with 1 whole olive secured with a toothpick or decorative pick.

1 APPETIZER: Calories 130; Total Fat 8g (Saturated Fat 3.5g; Trans Fat 0g); Cholesterol 15mg; Sodium 290mg; Total Carbohydrate 9g (Dietary Fiber 1g); Protein 3g **EXCHANGES:** ½ Starch, 2 Fat **CARBOHYDRATE CHOICES:** ½

speed it up

To quickly soften cream cheese, use your microwave. Remove the foil wrapper and place the cream cheese in a microwavable bowl. Microwave uncovered on medium (50%) 45 to 60 seconds for a 3-ounce package of cream cheese.

20 minutes or less

mini crab points

PREP TIME **15 MINUTES**   START TO FINISH **15 MINUTES**   **16 APPETIZERS**

¼ **cup mayonnaise or salad dressing**

1 **small clove garlic, finely chopped**

1 **can (6 oz) crabmeat, well drained, flaked**

¼ **cup finely chopped celery**

2 **tablespoons diced red bell pepper**

2 **medium green onions, thinly sliced (2 tablespoons)**

¼ **teaspoon seafood seasoning (from 6-oz container)**

4 **slices whole wheat bread, toasted**

Chopped fresh parsley

1 In medium bowl, mix mayonnaise and garlic. Stir in crabmeat, celery, bell pepper, onions and seafood seasoning.

2 Top toasted bread with crab mixture. Cut diagonally into quarters. Sprinkle with parsley.

1 APPETIZER: Calories 50; Total Fat 3g (Saturated Fat 0.5g; Trans Fat 0g); Cholesterol 10mg; Sodium 100mg; Total Carbohydrate 4g (Dietary Fiber 0g); Protein 3g **EXCHANGES:** ½ Starch, ½ Fat **CARBOHYDRATE CHOICES:** 0

instant success

If you have leafy tips handy after chopping the celery, you can use them instead of the parsley to garnish the appetizers.

20 minutes or less

egg salad–salami sandwiches

PREP TIME **10 MINUTES**   START TO FINISH **10 MINUTES**   8 SERVINGS (½ SANDWICH EACH)

½   pint (about 1¼ cups) egg salad (from deli)

¼   cup finely chopped cucumber

¼   cup thinly sliced halved radishes

2   tablespoons chopped fresh chives

8   slices rye-and-pumpernickel swirl bread

¼   cup horseradish mustard

4   large butterhead lettuce leaves, torn to fit bread

12   thin slices Genoa salami (about 4 oz)

1 In small bowl, stir together egg salad, cucumber, radishes and chives until blended. On one side of each bread slice, spread 1½ teaspoons mustard.

2 To make sandwiches, top each of 4 bread slices, mustard side up, with 1 lettuce leaf, about ⅓ cup egg salad mixture and 3 slices salami, loosely folded in half. Top with remaining bread slices, mustard side down. To serve, cut sandwiches in half.

1 SERVING: Calories 210; Total Fat 13g (Saturated Fat 3g; Trans Fat 0g); Cholesterol 100mg; Sodium 620mg; Total Carbohydrate 15g (Dietary Fiber 1g); Protein 8g **EXCHANGES:** 1 Starch, ½ Medium-Fat Meat, 2 Fat **CARBOHYDRATE CHOICES:** 1

speed it up

Purchased egg salad is a real time-saver for this recipe. Look for it near the deli counter or salad bar at your grocery store. If you don't see it out, don't give up. Inquire at the deli counter—they may keep it refrigerated behind the counter rather than in the deli case.

20 minutes or less
muffuletta slices

PREP TIME **15 MINUTES**   START TO FINISH **15 MINUTES**   **18 SERVINGS**

1   loaf (20 inches) baguette French bread, cut in half horizontally

¼   cup chive-and-onion cream cheese spread (from 8-oz container)

1   jar (6 to 7 oz) marinated artichoke hearts, well drained, patted dry, finely chopped

¼   cup basil pesto

½   cup roasted red bell peppers (from 12-oz jar), patted dry, cut into strips

¼   lb thinly sliced salami

18   pitted kalamata olives

18   pimiento-stuffed green olives

1 Remove some of the soft bread from center of top half of baguette to make a long, narrow well.

2 In small bowl, mix cream cheese spread and artichokes. Generously spread mixture in long, narrow well in top half of baguette. Spread pesto over cream cheese mixture.

3 Place roasted pepper strips on bottom half of baguette. Fold salami slices in half; layer diagonally over peppers, overlapping slices slightly.

4 Place top half of baguette, pesto side down, over salami; press halves together well. Thread 1 kalamata and 1 green olive onto each of 18 toothpicks or cocktail picks; insert toothpicks through all layers of sandwich at 1-inch intervals. Cut between toothpicks into 18 slices.

1 SERVING: Calories 140; Total Fat 6g (Saturated Fat 2g; Trans Fat 0g); Cholesterol 10mg; Sodium 380mg; Total Carbohydrate 16g (Dietary Fiber 1g); Protein 5g **EXCHANGES:** 1 Starch, 1 Fat **CARBOHYDRATE CHOICES:** 1

make it ahead

This appetizer loaf can be assembled several hours ahead. Wrap it tightly in plastic wrap and refrigerate until you're ready to cut and serve.

20 minutes or less

hummus and cucumber bites

PREP TIME **15 MINUTES**   START TO FINISH **15 MINUTES**   **16 APPETIZERS**

2   pita (pocket) breads (6 inches)

⅔   cup roasted red pepper hummus (from 7-oz container)

⅓   English (seedless) cucumber (about 4 inches)

½   teaspoon smoked Spanish paprika

16   sprigs fresh dill weed

1 Cut each pita bread into 8 wedges. Spread about 1 teaspoon hummus on each wedge.

2 Score cucumber peel lengthwise with tines of fork. Cut cucumber in half lengthwise. Cut each half crosswise into 16 thin slices. Place 2 half-slices cucumber on hummus on each bite.

3 Sprinkle with paprika. Garnish with dill weed.

1 APPETIZER: Calories 40; Total Fat 1g (Saturated Fat 0g; Trans Fat 0g); Cholesterol 0mg; Sodium 70mg; Total Carbohydrate 6g (Dietary Fiber 0g); Protein 1g **EXCHANGES:** ½ Starch **CARBOHYDRATE CHOICES:** ½

instant success

Smoked Spanish paprika has a smoky, spicy flavor, but you can use regular paprika instead.

20 minutes or less

layered mediterranean tuna spread

PREP TIME **15 MINUTES**   START TO FINISH **15 MINUTES**   **16 SERVINGS (¼ CUP SPREAD AND 3 CRACKERS EACH)**

1 **container (8 oz) chive-and-onion cream cheese spread**

1 **shallot, finely chopped**

1 **teaspoon Italian seasoning**

½ **cup pitted niçoise or kalamata olives, cut in half**

1 **can (5 oz) albacore tuna, well drained, broken into chunks**

1 **medium tomato, seeded, coarsely chopped**

1 **hard-cooked egg, finely chopped**

1 **tablespoon chopped fresh parsley**

48 **crackers**

1 In small bowl, mix cream cheese, shallot and Italian seasoning until well blended. Spread in 8-inch circle on serving plate.

2 Top with olives, tuna, tomato, egg and parsley. Serve with crackers.

1 SERVING: Calories 110; Total Fat 7g (Saturated Fat 3g; Trans Fat 0g); Cholesterol 30mg; Sodium 220mg; Total Carbohydrate 7g (Dietary Fiber 0g); Protein 5g **EXCHANGES:** ½ Starch, ½ Lean Meat, 1 Fat **CARBOHYDRATE CHOICES:** ½

speed it up

Save time by purchasing the hard-cooked egg from your grocery store's deli.

20 minutes or less

caribbean layered dip

PREP TIME **20 MINUTES**   START TO FINISH **20 MINUTES**   24 SERVINGS (2 TABLESPOONS DIP AND 3 CHIPS EACH)

- 1 **package (8 oz) cream cheese, softened**
- ½ **cup sour cream**
- 1 **tablespoon taco seasoning mix (from 1-oz package)**
- 1 **can (15 oz) black beans, drained, rinsed**
- ½ **cup chopped red bell pepper**
- ½ **cup chopped mango**
- 2 **tablespoons chopped fresh cilantro**
- 1 **to 2 teaspoons finely chopped jalapeño chiles**

   Lime-flavored or plain tortilla chips

1 In small bowl, mix cream cheese, sour cream and taco seasoning mix with spoon or electric mixer on medium speed until well mixed. On 10-inch round serving plate, spread cream cheese mixture.

2 Sprinkle black beans, bell pepper, mango, cilantro and chiles over cream cheese mixture. Serve immediately, or cover with plastic wrap and refrigerate until serving time. Serve with tortilla chips.

1 SERVING: Calories 90; Total Fat 6g (Saturated Fat 3g, Trans Fat 0g); Cholesterol 15mg; Sodium 150mg; Total Carbohydrate 9g (Dietary Fiber 1g); Protein 3g **EXCHANGES:** ½ Starch, 1 Fat **CARBOHYDRATE CHOICES:** ½

make it ahead

Save on last-minute fussing. Make this layered dip up to 4 hours ahead; cover tightly and refrigerate.

quick chicken quesadillas

PREP TIME **25 MINUTES**   START TO FINISH **25 MINUTES**   **8 SERVINGS (½ QUESADILLA EACH)**

1 **package (6 oz) refrigerated cooked Southwest-flavor chicken breast strips**

½ **cup chunky-style salsa**

8 **flour tortillas (6 to 8 inches)**

 Cooking spray

2 **cups finely shredded Colby–Monterey Jack cheese blend (8 oz)**

¼ **cup sour cream**

 Additional chunky-style salsa, if desired

1 Cut chicken into bite-size pieces. In small bowl, mix chicken and salsa.

2 Spray one side of 1 tortilla with cooking spray; place sprayed side down in 10-inch skillet. Layer with one-quarter of the chicken mixture and ½ cup of the cheese. Top with another tortilla; spray top of tortilla with cooking spray.

3 Cook uncovered over medium heat 4 to 6 minutes, carefully turning after 2 minutes, until golden brown and cheese is melted. Repeat with remaining tortillas, chicken mixture and cheese. To serve, cut quesadillas into wedges. Serve with sour cream and salsa.

1 SERVING: Calories 300; Total Fat 15g (Saturated Fat 8g; Trans Fat 1g); Cholesterol 45mg; Sodium 770mg; Total Carbohydrate 26g (Dietary Fiber 1g); Protein 15g **EXCHANGES:** 1½ Starch, 1 Very Lean Meat, ½ High-Fat Meat, 2 Fat **CARBOHYDRATE CHOICES:** 2

instant success

Can't find the refrigerated seasoned chicken? Substitute 1½ cups chopped rotisserie or other cooked chicken.

20 minutes or less

goat cheese quesadillas

PREP TIME **20 MINUTES**   START TO FINISH **20 MINUTES**   **12 SERVINGS**

4   flour tortillas (8 inches)

¼   cup thinly sliced fresh basil leaves

1   cup frozen cooked deveined peeled small shrimp, thawed, patted dry, coarsely chopped

¼   cup crumbled chèvre (goat) cheese (1 oz)

⅓   cup chopped drained roasted red bell peppers (from a jar)

¾   cup shredded mozzarella cheese (3 oz)

2   tablespoons butter

1 Place tortillas on work surface; arrange basil, shrimp, chèvre cheese, red bell peppers and mozzarella cheese evenly over half of each tortilla. Fold tortillas over filling, pressing gently.

2 In 10-inch skillet, melt 1½ teaspoons butter over medium heat, rotating skillet to coat evenly. Place 2 quesadillas in skillet; spread tops with 1½ teaspoons butter. Cook 2 to 3 minutes or until light golden brown. Turn carefully; cook 2 to 3 minutes longer or until light golden brown. Remove from skillet; keep warm. Repeat with remaining 1 tablespoon butter and 2 quesadillas.

3 To serve, cut each quesadilla into 3 wedges.

1 SERVING: Calories 110; Total Fat 6g (Saturated Fat 3g; Trans Fat 0g); Cholesterol 35mg; Sodium 200mg; Total Carbohydrate 9g (Dietary Fiber 0g); Protein 6g **EXCHANGES:** ½ Starch, ½ Lean Meat, 1 Fat **CARBOHYDRATE CHOICES:** ½

speed it up

An easy way to slice basil is to stack up the leaves, then roll them up lengthwise. Using a sharp knife, cut basil rolls crosswise into thin strips.

20 minutes or less

skillet chicken nachos

PREP TIME **20 MINUTES**   START TO FINISH **20 MINUTES**   **6 SERVINGS**

1   tablespoon olive or vegetable oil

1¼ lb boneless skinless chicken breasts, cut into ¼-inch pieces

1   package (1 oz) taco seasoning mix

1   can (8 oz) tomato sauce

1   medium red bell pepper, chopped (1 cup)

1   can (15 oz) black beans, drained, rinsed

1   can (7 oz) whole kernel sweet corn, drained

2   cups shredded Mexican cheese blend (8 oz)

6   oz tortilla chips (about 42 chips)

¼   cup chopped fresh cilantro

1 In 12-inch nonstick skillet, heat oil over medium-high heat. Cook chicken in oil 3 to 5 minutes, stirring occasionally, until no longer pink in center.

2 Stir in taco seasoning mix, tomato sauce, bell pepper, beans, corn and 1 cup of the cheese. Reduce heat to medium; cook 3 to 5 minutes, stirring occasionally, until thoroughly heated and cheese is melted.

3 Divide tortilla chips among 6 plates. Spoon chicken mixture evenly over chips. Sprinkle with remaining 1 cup cheese and the cilantro.

1 SERVING: Calories 520; Total Fat 24g (Saturated Fat 9g; Trans Fat 0g); Cholesterol 95mg; Sodium 1320mg; Total Carbohydrate 38g (Dietary Fiber 5g); Protein 36g **EXCHANGES:** 2 Starch, ½ Other Carbohydrate, ½ Vegetable, 4 Very Lean Meat, 4 Fat **CARBOHYDRATE CHOICES:** 2½

instant success

For Skillet Beef Nachos, substitute 1¼ pounds ground beef for the chicken. In step 1, cook beef 5 to 7 minutes or until thoroughly cooked. Drain and proceed as directed.

chewy pizza bread

PREP TIME **10 MINUTES**   START TO FINISH **30 MINUTES**   **16 SERVINGS**

1½ cups all-purpose flour

1½ teaspoons baking powder

½ teaspoon salt

¾ cup regular or nonalcoholic beer

½ cup tomato pasta sauce

⅓ cup shredded mozzarella cheese

1 tablespoon chopped fresh basil leaves, if desired

1 Heat oven to 425°F. Spray 8-inch square pan with cooking spray.

2 In medium bowl, mix flour, baking powder and salt. Stir in beer just until flour is moistened. Spread dough in pan. Spread pasta sauce over dough. Sprinkle with cheese.

3 Bake 15 to 20 minutes or until toothpick inserted in center comes out clean. Sprinkle with basil. Cut into 2-inch squares. Serve warm.

1 SERVING: Calories 60; Total Fat 1g (Saturated Fat 0g; Trans Fat 0g); Cholesterol 0mg; Sodium 170mg; Total Carbohydrate 11g (Dietary Fiber 0g); Protein 2g **EXCHANGES:** ½ Starch **CARBOHYDRATE CHOICES:** 1

easy add-on

Pepperoni? Yes, go ahead and add slices of pepperoni on the sauce before topping with cheese.

20 minutes or less
loaded mini dogs

PREP TIME **20 MINUTES**   START TO FINISH **20 MINUTES**   **12 SERVINGS**

½ cup yellow mustard

¼ cup apple cider vinegar

3 tablespoons brown sugar

24 cocktail-size hot dogs
(from 14-oz package)

12 mini burger buns (about
2½ inches in diameter)

½ cup pickle relish

½ cup chopped tomato

¼ cup chopped onion

1 In 1½-quart saucepan, heat mustard, vinegar and sugar about 3 minutes over medium heat, stirring frequently, until sugar is dissolved. Add hot dogs; cover and cook 5 minutes, stirring frequently, until heated through.

2 Meanwhile, slice buns horizontally nearly in half. To serve, fill each bun with 2 hot dogs, 1 teaspoon mustard sauce, 2 teaspoons relish, 2 teaspoons tomato and 1 teaspoon onion.

1 SERVING: Calories 170; Total Fat 7g (Saturated Fat 2.5g; Trans Fat 0g); Cholesterol 10mg; Sodium 550mg; Total Carbohydrate 20g (Dietary Fiber 1g); Protein 4g **EXCHANGES:** 1 Starch, ½ Other Carbohydrate, 1½ Fat **CARBOHYDRATE CHOICES:** 1

easy add-on

For some extra-spicy crunch, top loaded dogs with sliced pepperoncini peppers.

mini greek-style topped potatoes

PREP TIME **10 MINUTES**   START TO FINISH **30 MINUTES**   **24 APPETIZERS**

12 small red potatoes

2 tablespoons zesty Italian dressing

½ teaspoon garlic salt

½ cup crumbled tomato-basil feta cheese (2 oz)

½ cup chopped drained roasted red bell peppers (from a jar)

¼ cup chopped pitted kalamata olives

¼ teaspoon crushed red pepper flakes

2 tablespoons chopped fresh chives

1 Heat oven to 450°F. Cut each potato in half; place in medium bowl. Toss potatoes with 1 tablespoon of the dressing. On cookie sheet, place potatoes, cut side up. (If potatoes don't sit flat, cut off thin slice from underside.) Sprinkle potatoes with garlic salt. Bake 15 to 20 minutes or until tender when pierced with a fork. Cool 5 minutes.

2 Meanwhile, in small bowl, stir together remaining 1 tablespoon dressing and the remaining ingredients. For each appetizer, spoon about 1 heaping teaspoon topping on 1 potato half.

1 APPETIZER: Calories 80; Total Fat 1.5g (Saturated Fat 0g; Trans Fat 0g); Cholesterol 0mg; Sodium 95mg; Total Carbohydrate 15g (Dietary Fiber 1g); Protein 2g **EXCHANGES:** 1 Starch **CARBOHYDRATE CHOICES:** 1

speed it up

Pitted olives can be found at the grocery store in the olive or salad bar, or in jars near the other condiments. Starting with pitted olives makes chopping them much quicker.

20 minutes or less

bacon-apple bruschetta

PREP TIME **20 MINUTES**   START TO FINISH **20 MINUTES**   **20 APPETIZERS**

20   slices (¼ inch thick) baguette French bread

1   tablespoon olive oil

3   slices thick-sliced bacon

1   unpeeled red cooking apple, coarsely chopped (about 2 cups)

3   medium green onions, sliced (3 tablespoons)

1   tablespoon sugar

1   tablespoon chopped fresh oregano leaves

5   slices (¾ oz each) sharp Cheddar cheese, cut into quarters

1 Set oven control to broil. Place bread slices on cookie sheet; brush tops with oil. Broil with tops 4 inches from heat 1 to 2 minutes or until lightly browned. Remove from oven; turn bread. Set aside.

2 In 10-inch skillet, cook bacon over medium-high heat about 6 minutes, turning occasionally, until crisp. Drain bacon on paper towels. Discard fat from skillet. Reduce heat to medium; cook apple in skillet 3 to 4 minutes, stirring occasionally, until almost tender. Add onions, sugar and oregano. Cook 3 to 4 minutes longer, stirring frequently, until apple is tender and starting to caramelize. Crumble bacon; add to apple mixture and heat through.

3 To make bruschetta, top untoasted side of each bread slice with 1 piece cheese and about 1 tablespoon apple mixture. Serve warm or at room temperature.

1 APPETIZER: Calories 110; Total Fat 3.5g (Saturated Fat 1.5g; Trans Fat 0g); Cholesterol 5mg; Sodium 220mg; Total Carbohydrate 16g (Dietary Fiber 1g); Protein 4g **EXCHANGES:** 1 Starch, ½ Fat **CARBOHYDRATE CHOICES:** 1

instant success

For a tasty alternative, substitute pumpernickel bread for the baguette French bread. Use either cocktail-size bread or regular-size pumpernickel bread sliced into quarters.

20 minutes or less

easy pizzettes

PREP TIME **10 MINUTES** START TO FINISH **20 MINUTES** **16 SERVINGS**

1 **cup pizza sauce**

8 **English muffins, split, toasted**

2 **cups shredded provolone cheese (8 oz)**

Assorted toppings (⅔ cup each sliced mushrooms, sliced ripe olives, chopped bell pepper and chopped red onion)

1 Heat oven to 425°F. Spread 1 tablespoon pizza sauce over each English muffin half. Sprinkle each with 1 tablespoon of the cheese. Arrange toppings on pizzas. Sprinkle with remaining cheese.

2 Place on ungreased cookie sheet. Bake 5 to 10 minutes or until cheese is melted.

1 SERVING: Calories 130; Total Fat 6g (Saturated Fat 2.5g; Trans Fat 0g); Cholesterol 10mg; Sodium 370mg; Total Carbohydrate 16g (Dietary Fiber 1g); Protein 6g **EXCHANGES:** 1 Starch, ½ High-Fat Meat **CARBOHYDRATE CHOICES:** 1

speed it up

Buy assorted pizza toppings from the salad bar at your grocery store—you can purchase just the amount you need.

spicy oven-fried chicken tenders with gorgonzola dip

PREP TIME **10 MINUTES**   START TO FINISH **25 MINUTES**
16 SERVINGS (1 TENDER AND 1 HEAPING TABLESPOON DIP EACH)

1 **cup sour cream**

2 **tablespoons fresh lemon juice**

1 **teaspoon ground red pepper (cayenne)**

1⅓ **cups Italian-style crispy bread crumbs**

1 **package (14 oz) chicken tenders, cut crosswise in half**

½ **cup mayonnaise or salad dressing**

½ **cup crumbled Gorgonzola cheese (2 oz)**

2 **tablespoons chopped fresh parsley**

1 **tablespoon milk**

1 Heat oven to 400°F. Spray large cookie sheet with cooking spray. In small shallow bowl, stir together ½ cup of the sour cream, 1 tablespoon of the lemon juice and ½ teaspoon of the red pepper until blended. In 1-gallon resealable food-storage plastic bag, combine bread crumbs and ¼ teaspoon of the red pepper.

2 Dip chicken pieces in sour cream mixture. Place 4 at a time in bag with bread crumbs. Seal bag; shake to coat. Place coated chicken on cookie sheet. Repeat with remaining chicken, sour cream mixture and bread crumbs. Bake 12 to 15 minutes or until chicken is no longer pink in center and coating is golden brown.

3 Meanwhile, in small bowl, stir together remaining ½ cup sour cream, 1 tablespoon lemon juice, ¼ teaspoon red pepper, the mayonnaise, cheese and parsley until blended; stir in milk. Serve dip with tenders.

1 SERVING: Calories 150; Total Fat 10g (Saturated Fat 3.5g; Trans Fat 0g); Cholesterol 25mg; Sodium 290mg; Total Carbohydrate 8g (Dietary Fiber 0g); Protein 8g **EXCHANGES:** ½ Starch, 1 Very Lean Meat, 2 Fat **CARBOHYDRATE CHOICES:** ½

make it ahead

You can make this recipe ahead to take the pressure off mealtime. Make the dip as directed, cover and refrigerate for up to 1 day. Make the chicken tenders just to the point of baking. Cover and refrigerate for up to 4 hours. Uncover and bake them right before serving.

grilled veggies and steak

PREP TIME **20 MINUTES**   START TO FINISH **30 MINUTES**   **4 SERVINGS**

⅔ cup balsamic vinaigrette dressing

1 package (6 oz) small fresh portabella mushrooms

½ lb beef sirloin steak (about ¾ inch thick), cut into ¾-inch cubes

1 cup frozen pearl onions (from 1-lb bag), thawed

½ cup halved grape or cherry tomatoes

1 Heat gas or charcoal grill. Reserve 2 tablespoons of the vinaigrette; set aside. In large bowl, place mushrooms, beef, onions and remaining vinaigrette; toss to coat. Let stand 10 minutes; drain. Place mixture in grill basket (grill "wok"). Place basket on cookie sheet to catch drips while carrying to grill.

2 Place basket on grill. Cover grill; cook over medium-high heat 7 to 9 minutes, shaking basket or stirring beef mixture twice, until vegetables are tender and beef is desired doneness. Stir in tomatoes.

3 Spoon beef mixture into serving dish. Stir in reserved 2 tablespoons vinaigrette.

1 SERVING: Calories 150; Total Fat 5g (Saturated Fat 1g; Trans Fat 0g); Cholesterol 30mg; Sodium 350mg; Total Carbohydrate 10g (Dietary Fiber 1g); Protein 15g **EXCHANGES:** 1 Vegetable, 2 Very Lean Meat, 1 Fat **CARBOHYDRATE CHOICES:** ½

make it a meal

Throw in a ciabatta loaf or some petits pains, and maybe a jar of store-bought tapenade spread for a light summertime dinner.

20 minutes or less

bbq chipotle chicken–cheddar sliders

PREP TIME **20 MINUTES**   START TO FINISH **20 MINUTES**   **12 SANDWICHES**

1 cup barbecue sauce

2 tablespoons chopped fresh cilantro

1 chipotle chile in adobo sauce, finely chopped (from 7-oz can)

3 cups chopped cooked chicken

1 package (15 oz) slider buns (12 buns)

3 cups mixed baby greens (from 5-oz package)

3 slices (¾ oz each) sharp Cheddar cheese, cut into quarters

36 dill pickle or jalapeño kettle-cooked potato chips

1 In 2-quart saucepan, heat barbecue sauce, cilantro and chile to boiling over medium heat, stirring frequently. Stir in chicken. Heat to boiling; reduce heat. Cover and simmer about 5 minutes, stirring occasionally, until heated through.

2 For each sandwich, layer bottom half of bun with about ¼ cup baby greens, ¼ cup chicken mixture, 1 piece cheese and 3 potato chips; cover with top half of bun.

1 SANDWICH: Calories 240; Total Fat 7g (Saturated Fat 2g; Trans Fat 0g); Cholesterol 35mg; Sodium 500mg; Total Carbohydrate 30g (Dietary Fiber 1g); Protein 15g **EXCHANGES:** 2 Starch, 1½ Very Lean Meat, 1 Fat **CARBOHYDRATE CHOICES:** 2

instant success

If you like, you can use mini dinner rolls in place of the slider buns. Look for rolls that are 2 to 3 inches in diameter. Cut each crosswise in half.

california sliders

PREP TIME **30 MINUTES**   START TO FINISH **30 MINUTES**   **16 SANDWICHES**

1   lb lean (at least 80%)
    ground beef

2   teaspoons dried minced onion

1   teaspoon parsley flakes

¾   teaspoon seasoned salt

4   slices (1 oz each) American
    cheese, cut into quarters

4   burger buns, cut into quarters

16   thin slices plum (Roma)
    tomatoes (2 small), if desired

16   thin hamburger-style dill pickle
    slices, if desired

    Ketchup, if desired

    Mustard, if desired

1 Heat gas or charcoal grill. In medium bowl, mix beef, onion, parsley and seasoned salt. Divide into 16 portions. Shape each portion into a ball and flatten to ½-inch-thick patty about 1½ inches in diameter. On each of 4 (12-inch) metal skewers, thread 4 patties horizontally, or place in grill basket.

2 Place patties on grill. Cover grill; cook over medium heat 8 to 10 minutes, turning once, until meat thermometer inserted in center of patties reads 160°F.

3 Remove burgers from skewers. Immediately top each with piece of cheese. Place each burger in bun quarter with tomato slice. Place pickle slice on top; spear with toothpick to hold layers together. Serve with ketchup and mustard for dipping.

1 SANDWICH: Calories 110; Total Fat 6g (Saturated Fat 2.5g; Trans Fat 0g); Cholesterol 25mg; Sodium 270mg; Total Carbohydrate 7g (Dietary Fiber 0g); Protein 8g **EXCHANGES:** ½ Starch, 1 Medium-Fat Meat **CARBOHYDRATE CHOICES:** ½

instant success

To broil the patties, set the oven control to broil. Thread the patties on skewers as directed. Place the patties on a rack in a broiler pan. Broil with tops 6 inches from the heat 8 to 10 minutes, turning once, until no longer pink in the center (160°F).

grilled stuffed pepper wedges

PREP TIME **25 MINUTES**   START TO FINISH **25 MINUTES**   **8 SERVINGS (2 WEDGES EACH)**

½ **cup chive-and-onion cream cheese spread (from 8-oz container)**

1 **tablespoon chopped ripe olives**

1 **medium green bell pepper, cut into 8 wedges**

1 **medium red bell pepper, cut into 8 wedges**

3 **tablespoons finely shredded Cheddar-American cheese blend**

1 Heat gas or charcoal grill. In small bowl, mix cream cheese and olives.

2 Spread about 2 teaspoons cream cheese mixture inside each pepper wedge. Sprinkle with shredded cheese.

3 Place on grill, cheese sides up, over medium heat. Cover grill; cook 8 to 10 minutes or until bottoms of peppers are blistered and charred and cheese is melted.

1 SERVING: Calories 60; Total Fat 5g (Saturated Fat 3.5g; Trans Fat 0g); Cholesterol 15mg; Sodium 150mg; Total Carbohydrate 3g (Dietary Fiber 0g); Protein 2g **EXCHANGES:** 1½ Fat **CARBOHYDRATE CHOICES:** 0

speed it up

Up to 2 hours ahead, spread pepper wedges with cream cheese mixture, and refrigerate. Sprinkle with cheese before grilling.

margarita shrimp kabobs

PREP TIME **25 MINUTES**   START TO FINISH **25 MINUTES**   **8 SERVINGS**

1 teaspoon grated lime zest

¼ cup fresh lime juice

2 cloves garlic, finely chopped

2 tablespoons tequila, if desired

¼ teaspoon salt

1 lb uncooked deveined peeled large shrimp (about 24), thawed if frozen, tail shells removed

1 medium zucchini, cut into ½-inch slices

1 large red bell pepper, cut into bite-size pieces

1 tablespoon olive or vegetable oil

1 Heat gas or charcoal grill. Carefully brush oil on grill rack. In large resealable food-storage plastic bag, mix lime zest, lime juice, garlic, tequila and salt; add shrimp. Seal bag, squeezing out air; turn to coat shrimp. Let stand 10 minutes to marinate. Drain shrimp; discard marinade.

2 On each of 8 (12-inch) metal skewers, alternately thread shrimp, zucchini and bell pepper, leaving ¼-inch space between each piece. Brush with 1 tablespoon oil.

3 Place kabobs on grill over medium-high heat. Cover grill; cook 5 to 6 minutes, turning once, until shrimp are pink and vegetables are crisp-tender.

1 SERVING: Calories 70; Total Fat 2.5g (Saturated Fat 0g; Trans Fat 0g); Cholesterol 80mg; Sodium 170mg; Total Carbohydrate 3g (Dietary Fiber 0g); Protein 9g **EXCHANGES:** 1 Lean Meat **CARBOHYDRATE CHOICES:** 0

make it a meal

Serve the kabobs with warm whole wheat pita bread and a garden salad on the side.

bacon-wrapped chicken sausage kabobs

PREP TIME **25 MINUTES**   START TO FINISH **25 MINUTES**   **8 SERVINGS**

KABOBS

- 1 **package (12 oz) fully cooked smoked chicken and apple sausages (4 per package)**
- 1 **package (2.1 oz) precooked bacon, cut into thirds**
- 2 **medium zucchini, cut into ¾-inch slices (16 slices)**
- 16 **cherry tomatoes**
- 3 **scallions, cut into 2-inch pieces (8 pieces)**

GLAZE

- ½ **cup chili sauce**
- 3 **tablespoons Italian dressing**

1 Heat gas or charcoal grill. Cut sausages crosswise into fourths; wrap 1 piece of bacon around each sausage. On each of 8 (9-inch) metal skewers, alternately thread 1 bacon-wrapped sausage (make sure bacon is secured to sausage with skewer), 1 zucchini slice, 1 cherry tomato, 1 scallion piece, 1 cherry tomato, 1 zucchini slice and 1 bacon-wrapped sausage.

2 In small bowl, combine glaze ingredients; reserve half.

3 Place kabobs on grill over medium-high heat. Cover grill; cook 5 to 6 minutes, basting with remaining glaze and turning every minute, until zucchini is tender. Remove kabobs from grill; brush with reserved glaze.

1 SERVING: Calories 180; Total Fat 10g (Saturated Fat 3g; Trans Fat 0g); Cholesterol 45mg; Sodium 790mg; Total Carbohydrate 10g (Dietary Fiber 2g); Protein 12g **EXCHANGES:** ½ Starch, ½ Vegetable, 1½ Medium-Fat Meat, ½ Fat **CARBOHYDRATE CHOICES:** ½

make it a meal

Serve the kabobs with some herbed rice and a crisp lettuce salad for an easy, mouthwatering meal.

skillet chicken in a flash!

With just a few ingredients and less than 20 minutes, you can have great-tasting chicken on the table—it's that easy and that quick. Just follow these easy directions and pick a flavor from the delicious choices below.

- *Start with 4 boneless skinless chicken breasts.*
- *Flatten each to about ¼-inch thickness between sheets of plastic wrap or waxed paper using the flat side of a meat mallet or a rolling pin.*
- *Use a 12-inch nonstick skillet and follow directions below using medium heat. Chicken is done when juices of chicken is clear when center of thickest part is cut (at least 165°F).*

1 Buffalo Chicken: Heat 1 tablespoon vegetable oil in skillet. Add chicken; brown on both sides. Pour ½ cup buffalo-chicken-wing-flavored sauce evenly over chicken; turn to coat. Cook about 8 minutes, turning once. During last 2 to 3 minutes of cooking, sprinkle each chicken breast with about 2 teaspoons crumbled blue cheese.

2 Caesar-Feta Chicken: Heat ¼ cup vinaigrette-style Caesar dressing in skillet. Add chicken; cook about 10 minutes, turning once. During last 2 to 3 minutes of cooking, sprinkle chicken with 1 cup cut-up seeded tomato and ½ cup crumbled feta cheese; cover skillet to soften cheese.

3 Fresh Herb Chicken: Heat 1 tablespoon butter in skillet. Add chicken; brown both sides. Add ¼ cup dry white wine or chicken broth, 1 tablespoon each chopped fresh basil, chives and dill, and ¼ teaspoon garlic salt. Cook about 8 minutes, turning once.

4 Italian Chicken and Peppers: Heat ¼ cup vinaigrette-style Italian dressing in skillet. Add chicken; cook about 10 minutes, turning once. During last 5 minutes of cooking, add 2 small bell peppers (any color), cut into strips; stir once or twice.

5 Pecan-Maple Chicken: Melt 2 table-spoons butter with ½ teaspoon salt in skillet. Add chicken; brown on both sides. Add 2 tablespoons pure maple syrup and ½ cup pecan halves. Cook about 8 minutes, turning chicken once and pecans twice.

6 Ranch Chicken: Heat 2 tablespoons vegetable oil in skillet. Brush chicken with ¼ cup ranch dressing; coat evenly with ⅓ cup Italian style crispy bread crumbs. Cook about 10 minutes, turning once.

7 *(no photo)* **Chicken in Curry Sauce:** Heat 1 tablespoon vegetable oil in skillet. Sprinkle chicken with ½ teaspoon garlic pepper Brown chicken on both sides. Stir in 1 cup frozen peas, ½ cup red curry sauce and ¼ cup water. Cook 8 to 10 minutes over medium-low heat until peas are tender, stirring once or twice. Sprinkle with chopped fresh cilantro.

8 *(no photo)* **Fire Roasted Chicken and Zucchini:** Heat 1 tablespoon vegetable oil in skillet. Sprinkle chicken with ½ teaspoon garlic salt and ½ teaspoon dried oregano leaves. Brown chicken on both sides. Add 1 can (14 ounces) fire roasted diced tomatoes and 1 medium zucchini, sliced. Cook 8 to 10 minutes over medium-low heat, turning chicken and stirring once or twice until zucchini is tender.

chicken+turkey

20 minutes or less

taco chicken with corn salsa

PREP TIME **20 MINUTES**   START TO FINISH **20 MINUTES**   **4 SERVINGS**

1 **package (1 oz) taco seasoning mix**

4 **boneless skinless chicken breasts (about 1¼ lb)**

2 **tablespoons vegetable oil**

1 **can (11 oz) whole kernel corn with red and green peppers, drained**

1 **medium avocado, pitted, peeled and chopped**

2 **tablespoons finely chopped red onion**

2 **tablespoons chopped fresh cilantro**

1 **tablespoon fresh lime juice**

1 **teaspoon honey**

1 In medium bowl, reserve 2 teaspoons of the taco seasoning mix. Place remaining taco seasoning mix in shallow dish. Add chicken; turn to coat with seasoning mix.

2 In 12-inch skillet, heat oil over medium heat. Cook chicken in oil 3 to 5 minutes, turning once, until brown. Reduce heat to medium-low. Cook about 8 minutes, turning once, or until juice of chicken is clear when center of thickest part is cut (at least 165°F).

3 Meanwhile, add remaining ingredients to reserved taco seasoning mix; toss gently. Serve salsa with chicken.

1 SERVING: Calories 410; Total Fat 18g (Saturated Fat 3.5g; Trans Fat 0g); Cholesterol 85mg; Sodium 690mg; Total Carbohydrate 26g (Dietary Fiber 5g); Protein 35g **EXCHANGES:** 1 Starch, ½ Other Carbohydrate, 4½ Very Lean Meat, 3 Fat **CARBOHYDRATE CHOICES:** 2

make it ahead

The lively salsa can be made ahead of time, but be sure to add the avocado just before serving to preserve its color and texture.

southwestern chicken scaloppine

PREP TIME **30 MINUTES**   START TO FINISH **30 MINUTES**   **4 SERVINGS**

4 boneless skinless chicken breasts (about 1¼ lb)

¼ cup all-purpose flour

1 teaspoon ground cumin

½ teaspoon salt

2 tablespoons vegetable oil

½ cup chicken broth

¼ teaspoon hot red pepper sauce, if desired

2 tablespoons fresh lime juice

2 tablespoons chopped fresh cilantro

1 Between pieces of plastic wrap or waxed paper, place chicken breast with smooth side down; gently pound with flat side of meat mallet or rolling pin until about ¼ inch thick. Repeat with remaining chicken. Cut chicken into smaller pieces if desired.

2 In shallow dish, mix flour, cumin and salt. Reserve 1 teaspoon mixture. Coat chicken with remaining flour mixture.

3 In 12-inch nonstick skillet, heat oil over medium heat. Add chicken; cook 3 to 5 minutes on each side or until golden brown and juice of chicken is clear when center of thickest part is cut (at least 165°F). Remove chicken from skillet; cover to keep warm.

4 In small bowl, stir reserved 1 teaspoon flour mixture into broth. Gradually stir broth mixture and red pepper sauce into skillet. Heat to boiling; stir in lime juice and cilantro. Serve sauce over chicken.

1 SERVING: Calories 260; Total Fat 12g (Saturated Fat 2.5g; Trans Fat 0g); Cholesterol 85mg; Sodium 500mg; Total Carbohydrate 7g (Dietary Fiber 0g); Protein 33g **EXCHANGES:** ½ Other Carbohydrate, 4½ Very Lean Meat, 2 Fat **CARBOHYDRATE CHOICES:** ½

make it a meal

Serve homemade or bakery cornbread or corn muffins, steamed broccoli and fresh fruit with the scaloppine for a scrumptious dinner.

feta-topped chicken

PREP TIME **25 MINUTES**   START TO FINISH **25 MINUTES**   **4 SERVINGS**

chicken + turkey

4 **boneless skinless chicken breasts (1¼ lb)**

2 **tablespoons balsamic vinaigrette dressing**

1 **teaspoon Italian seasoning**

¼ **teaspoon seasoned pepper blend**

1 **large plum (Roma) tomato, cut into 8 slices**

¼ **cup crumbled feta cheese (1 oz)**

1 Set oven control to broil. Spray rack of broiler pan with cooking spray. Brush both sides of chicken with dressing; sprinkle with Italian seasoning and seasoned pepper blend.

2 Place chicken on rack in pan. Broil with tops 4 inches from heat about 10 minutes, turning once, until juice of chicken is clear when center of thickest part is cut (at least 165°F).

3 Top each chicken breast with 2 slices tomato and 1 tablespoon cheese. Broil 2 to 3 minutes longer or until cheese is lightly browned.

1 SERVING: Calories 220; Total Fat 8g (Saturated Fat 2.5g; Trans Fat 0g); Cholesterol 90mg; Sodium 260mg; Total Carbohydrate 3g (Dietary Fiber 0g); Protein 33g **EXCHANGES:** 4½ Very Lean Meat, 1 Fat **CARBOHYDRATE CHOICES:** 0

instant success

Look for flavored feta cheese for a change of flavor. Or use crumbled blue cheese instead.

maple and rosemary–glazed chicken and carrots

PREP TIME **25 MINUTES**   START TO FINISH **25 MINUTES**   **4 SERVINGS**

2 cups ready-to-eat baby-cut carrots (from 16-oz bag)

⅓ cup maple syrup

1½ teaspoons finely chopped fresh rosemary or ½ teaspoon dried rosemary leaves

1 teaspoon grated orange zest

8 boneless skinless chicken thighs (1½ lb)

1 teaspoon seasoned salt

1 tablespoon olive oil

1. In 12-inch skillet, heat 2 tablespoons water to boiling. Add carrots; reduce heat to medium. Cover and simmer 5 minutes; drain.

2. Meanwhile, in small bowl, combine syrup, rosemary and orange zest.

3. Sprinkle chicken with seasoned salt. In same skillet, heat oil over medium heat. Cook carrots and chicken uncovered in oil about 5 minutes, turning chicken once, until chicken is brown. Add syrup mixture, stirring to coat. Cook 5 to 6 minutes longer, stirring occasionally, or until juice of chicken is clear when thickest part is cut (at least 165°F) and carrots are tender.

1 SERVING: Calories 390; Total Fat 17g (Saturated Fat 4.5g; Trans Fat 0g); Cholesterol 105mg; Sodium 490mg; Total Carbohydrate 24g (Dietary Fiber 2g); Protein 36g **EXCHANGES:** ½ Starch, 1 Other Carbohydrate, 1 Vegetable, 3 Lean Meat, 1½ Medium-Fat Meat **CARBOHYDRATE CHOICES:** 1½

speed it up

To quickly remove rosemary leaves from the stem, hold the top of the stem with your thumb and forefinger. With your other hand, run thumb and forefinger down the stem, stripping off the leaves.

barbecue chicken and vegetable supper

PREP TIME **25 MINUTES**   START TO FINISH **25 MINUTES**   **4 SERVINGS**

- **1** tablespoon vegetable oil
- **4** boneless skinless chicken breasts (1¼ lb)
- **½** teaspoon salt
- **2** cups frozen whole green beans (from 22-oz bag)
- **2** cups refrigerated red potato wedges (from 20-oz bag)
- **1** jar (12 oz) chicken gravy
- **⅓** cup barbecue sauce

1 In 12-inch nonstick skillet, heat oil over medium-high heat. Add chicken; sprinkle with salt. Cook 4 minutes, turning once, until browned.

2 Add beans, potatoes, gravy and barbecue sauce; stir to coat and mix. Cover; cook 5 to 8 minutes, stirring occasionally, until beans and potatoes are tender and juice of chicken is clear when center of thickest part is cut (at least 165°F).

1 SERVING: Calories 400; Total Fat 13g (Saturated Fat 3g; Trans Fat 0g); Cholesterol 85mg; Sodium 1220mg; Total Carbohydrate 33g (Dietary Fiber 6g); Protein 37g **EXCHANGES:** 1 Starch, 1 Other Carbohydrate, 1 Vegetable, 4½ Very Lean Meat, 2 Fat **CARBOHYDRATE CHOICES:** 2

instant success

Gravy lovers, this saucy skillet supper is your meal ticket! Try substituting frozen potato wedges or steak fries (no need to thaw first) if you can't find the refrigerated potato wedges.

chicken and ravioli carbonara

PREP TIME **30 MINUTES**   START TO FINISH **30 MINUTES**   **4 SERVINGS**

2 **tablespoons Italian dressing**

1 **lb boneless skinless chicken breasts, cut into 1-inch strips**

¾ **cup chicken broth**

1 **package (9 oz) refrigerated cheese-filled ravioli**

½ **cup half-and-half**

4 **slices bacon, crisply cooked, crumbled**

Shredded Parmesan cheese, if desired

Chopped fresh parsley, if desired

1 In 10-inch skillet, heat dressing over high heat. Cook chicken in dressing 2 to 4 minutes, turning occasionally, until brown and no longer pink in center.

2 Add broth and ravioli to skillet. Heat to boiling; reduce heat to medium. Cook uncovered 4 minutes or until ravioli are tender and almost all broth has evaporated.

3 Stir in half-and-half; reduce heat. Simmer uncovered 3 to 5 minutes or until sauce is hot and desired consistency (cook longer for a thicker sauce). Sprinkle with bacon, cheese and parsley.

1 SERVING: Calories 460; Total Fat 21g (Saturated Fat 9g; Trans Fat 0g); Cholesterol 125mg; Sodium 750mg; Total Carbohydrate 30g (Dietary Fiber 1g); Protein 38g **EXCHANGES:** 1 Starch, 1 Other Carbohydrate, 5 Very Lean Meat, 3½ Fat **CARBOHYDRATE CHOICES:** 2

instant success

The less time this sauce is cooked, the thinner it will be; if cooked longer, the sauce will become thick and coat the ravioli. The choice is yours—some people like to have more sauce to dip their bread into!

20 minutes or less

toasted pesto–chicken sausage sandwiches

PREP TIME **20 MINUTES**   START TO FINISH **20 MINUTES**   **4 SANDWICHES**

1 **package (12 oz) fully cooked smoked chicken and apple sausages (4 per package)**

3 **tablespoons olive oil**

½ **cup refrigerated basil pesto (from 7-oz container)**

2 **tablespoons mayonnaise or salad dressing**

8 **slices (½ inch thick) Italian bread**

4 **slices (¾ oz each) provolone cheese**

1 **large tomato, cut into 8 thin slices**

16 **fresh basil leaves**

1 Cut sausages almost in half crosswise, then in half lengthwise. In 12-inch skillet, heat 1 tablespoon of the oil over medium-high heat. Cook sausages in oil 5 to 7 minutes, turning occasionally, until golden brown. Remove from skillet; set aside.

2 Meanwhile, in small bowl, combine pesto and mayonnaise. Brush bread slices on one side with remaining 2 tablespoons oil. Turn 4 bread slices oiled side down; spread each with pesto-mayonnaise.

3 For each sandwich, top pesto-mayonnaise with 1 cheese slice, 2 tomato slices, 4 basil leaves, 1 cooked sausage and 1 bread slice, oiled side up. Heat same skillet or a griddle over medium-high heat. Cook sandwiches 3 to 5 minutes, turning once, until golden brown and cheese is melted.

1 SANDWICH: Calories 620; Total Fat 45g (Saturated Fat 11g; Trans Fat 0.5g); Cholesterol 80mg; Sodium 1340mg; Total Carbohydrate 28g (Dietary Fiber 2g); Protein 26g **EXCHANGES:** 1½ Starch, ½ Vegetable, 3 High-Fat Meat, 4 Fat **CARBOHYDRATE CHOICES:** 2

instant success

Cutting the sausages almost in half crosswise serves two purposes. First, they don't curl up while cooking, so they will lay flat in the sandwiches. Second, because the sausages are basically still in one long piece, they won't fall out of the bread when turning the sandwiches in the skillet.

20 minutes or less

chicken and black bean tostadas

PREP TIME **20 MINUTES**   START TO FINISH **20 MINUTES**   **6 SERVINGS**

1 **box (14 oz) enchilada dinner kit (6 soft tortillas, enchilada sauce and seasoning mix)**

2 **cups chopped or shredded deli rotisserie chicken (from 2-lb chicken)**

1 **package (8 oz) seasoned black beans**

½ **cup crumbled queso fresco cheese (2 oz)**

1 **small tomato, chopped (½ cup)**

   Fresh cilantro leaves, if desired

1 Heat oven to 375°F. Place tortillas (from dinner kit) on large cookie sheet. Spray both sides of tortillas with cooking spray. Bake 5 to 6 minutes, turning once, until lightly browned around edges.

2 Meanwhile, in 2-quart saucepan, mix chicken and black beans. Stir in seasoning mix and two-thirds of the enchilada sauce (from dinner kit). Cook over medium-low heat about 5 minutes, stirring occasionally, until hot.

3 On each tortilla, spread ⅓ cup chicken mixture; top with scant tablespoon of remaining enchilada sauce. Sprinkle with cheese and tomato. Garnish with cilantro leaves. Serve immediately.

1 SERVING: Calories 250; Total Fat 8g (Saturated Fat 2g; Trans Fat 1g); Cholesterol 45mg; Sodium 1310mg; Total Carbohydrate 28g (Dietary Fiber 3g); Protein 18g **EXCHANGES:** 2 Starch, 1½ Lean Meat, ½ Fat **CARBOHYDRATE CHOICES:** 2

speed it up

Rotisserie chicken is a great time-saver. Pick one up from the deli and pull all the meat off— you should get about 4 cups. Freeze it in 2-cup portions for use in recipes like this one.

betty crocker quick & easy   81

20 minutes or less

chicken and smoked provolone pizza

PREP TIME **10 MINUTES**   START TO FINISH **20 MINUTES**   **8 SERVINGS**

- 1   **package (14 oz) prebaked original Italian pizza crust (12 inches)**
- ¾   **cup chili sauce**
- 1½ **cups cut-up cooked chicken**
- 1   **teaspoon Montreal chicken or steak grill seasoning**
- 6   **oz smoked provolone cheese, shredded (1½ cups)**
- ¼   **small red onion, cut into thin rings**
- 2   **tablespoons chopped fresh cilantro**

1 Heat oven to 450°F. On ungreased cookie sheet, place pizza crust. Spread chili sauce over crust.

2 In small bowl, combine chicken and Montreal grill seasoning. Arrange chicken over chili sauce; top with cheese and onion.

3 Bake 8 to 10 minutes or until crust is golden brown and cheese is melted. Sprinkle with cilantro.

1 SERVING: Calories 280; Total Fat 10g (Saturated Fat 4.5g; Trans Fat 0g); Cholesterol 35mg; Sodium 920mg; Total Carbohydrate 28g (Dietary Fiber 2g); Protein 18g **EXCHANGES:** 2 Starch, 1½ Very Lean Meat, 1½ Fat **CARBOHYDRATE CHOICES:** 2

instant success

Mix and match the cheese and herbs for a different pizza every time! Use what you have on hand—try Monterey Jack, Cheddar or Havarti cheese instead of the provolone, and chopped fresh basil leaves or Italian (flat-leaf) parsley instead of the cilantro.

20 minutes or less

tangerine chicken stir-fry

PREP TIME **20 MINUTES**   START TO FINISH **20 MINUTES**   **4 SERVINGS**

½ **cup fresh tangerine or orange juice**

⅓ **cup soy sauce**

2 **teaspoons cornstarch**

1 **tablespoon peanut or canola oil**

1¼ **lb boneless skinless chicken breasts, cut into 1-inch pieces**

1 **cup ready-to-eat baby-cut carrots, cut in half lengthwise**

2 **cups fresh broccoli florets**

4 **oz whole fresh mushrooms, cut into quarters**

1 **can (8 oz) sliced water chestnuts, drained**

2 **tablespoons water**

¼ **cup finely chopped fresh cilantro**

Hot cooked rice, if desired

1 In small bowl, mix juice, soy sauce and cornstarch until cornstarch is dissolved; set aside.

2 In 12-inch wok or nonstick skillet, heat oil over medium-high heat. Cook chicken in oil 4 to 5 minutes, stirring frequently, until no longer pink in center. Add carrots; cook 2 to 3 minutes. Add broccoli, mushrooms, water chestnuts and water; cook 3 to 4 minutes longer, stirring frequently, until vegetables are crisp-tender.

3 Reduce heat to low. Stir juice mixture, then stir into chicken mixture. Cook and stir 1 minute or until sauce is slightly thickened. Sprinkle individual servings with 1 tablespoon cilantro. Serve with rice.

1 SERVING: Calories 290; Total Fat 8g (Saturated Fat 2g; Trans Fat 0g); Cholesterol 90mg; Sodium 1310mg; Total Carbohydrate 18g (Dietary Fiber 3g); Protein 36g **EXCHANGES:** ½ Starch, 2 Vegetable, 4½ Very Lean Meat, 1 Fat **CARBOHYDRATE CHOICES:** 1

instant success

The key to making a stir-fry is to cut meat and vegetables into similar sizes so they cook in about the same amount of time. Also, since the cooking goes quickly, always have the sauce ready before you start cooking. Stir the sauce before adding to the skillet to make sure the cornstarch is completely distributed.

caprese chicken

PREP TIME **25 MINUTES**   START TO FINISH **25 MINUTES**   **4 SERVINGS**

4 **boneless skinless chicken breasts (1¼ lb)**

1 **teaspoon Italian seasoning**

½ **teaspoon salt**

½ **teaspoon grated lemon zest**

1 **tablespoon olive oil**

1 **teaspoon balsamic vinegar**

1 **large plum (Roma) tomato, cut into 8 thin slices**

½ **cup shredded mozzarella cheese (2 oz)**

¼ **cup chopped fresh basil leaves**

Hot cooked linguine, if desired

1 Between pieces of plastic wrap or waxed paper, place each chicken breast smooth side down; gently pound with flat side of meat mallet or rolling pin until about ½ inch thick. In small bowl, mix Italian seasoning, salt and lemon zest; rub mixture evenly over smooth side of chicken.

2 In 10-inch nonstick skillet, heat oil and vinegar over medium-high heat. Add chicken, seasoned side down; cook 8 to 10 minutes, turning once, until juice of chicken is clear when center of thickest part is cut (at least 165°F).

3 Reduce heat to low. Top each chicken breast with 2 tomato slices and 2 tablespoons cheese. Cover; cook 2 minutes or until cheese is melted. Sprinkle with basil. Serve with linguine.

1 SERVING: Calories 250; Total Fat 11g (Saturated Fat 4g; Trans Fat 0g); Cholesterol 95mg; Sodium 460mg; Total Carbohydrate 2g (Dietary Fiber 0g); Protein 36g **EXCHANGES:** 4 Very Lean Meat, ½ Lean Meat, ½ Medium-Fat Meat, 1 Fat **CARBOHYDRATE CHOICES:** 0

make it a meal

Serve the chicken with a garden salad tossed with a light vinaigrette dressing.

20 minutes or less
chinese chicken stir-fry

PREP TIME **20 MINUTES**   START TO FINISH **20 MINUTES**   **3 SERVINGS**

1   tablespoon peanut oil

1   lb boneless skinless chicken
    breasts, cut into 1-inch pieces

1   cup frozen shelled edamame
    (green) soybeans (from 10- or
    12-oz bag), thawed

1   cup frozen sugar snap peas
    (from 24-oz bag), thawed

½   medium red bell pepper,
    cut into thin 2-inch strips
    (about 1 cup)

⅓   cup hoisin sauce

1   tablespoon soy sauce

1   teaspoon grated gingerroot

¾   teaspoon grated orange zest

1 In 12-inch wok or nonstick skillet, heat oil over medium-high heat. Cook chicken in oil 4 to 5 minutes, stirring occasionally, until no longer pink in center. Add edamame, snap peas and bell pepper; cook 2 to 3 minutes longer, stirring frequently, until vegetables are crisp-tender.

2 Stir in remaining ingredients. Cook and stir 1 minute or until hot.

1 SERVING: Calories 380; Total Fat 13g (Saturated Fat 2.5g; Trans Fat 0g); Cholesterol 95mg; Sodium 850mg; Total Carbohydrate 23g (Dietary Fiber 5g); Protein 42g **EXCHANGES:** 1 Starch, 1½ Vegetable, 5 Very Lean Meat, 2 Fat **CARBOHYDRATE CHOICES:** 1½

easy add-on

Like your stir-fry spicier? Just add ⅛ to ¼ teaspoon Thai chili sauce. It's available in the Asian food aisle.

20 minutes or less

coconut curry chicken

PREP TIME **20 MINUTES** START TO FINISH **20 MINUTES** **4 SERVINGS**

1 tablespoon curry powder

¾ lb boneless skinless chicken breasts

1 teaspoon vegetable oil

1 small onion, cut into 2 × ¼-inch strips

1 small zucchini, cut into ¼-inch slices

1 medium bell pepper (any color), cut into ¾-inch squares

⅓ cup light unsweetened coconut milk (not cream of coconut)

1 tablespoon brown bean sauce

1 teaspoon grated gingerroot

½ teaspoon salt

2 tablespoons shredded coconut, toasted

1 Rub curry powder on chicken. Cut chicken into ¾-inch pieces. Let stand 10 minutes.

2 Spray wok or 12-inch skillet with cooking spray; heat over medium-high heat until cooking spray starts to bubble. Add chicken; cook and stir 2 minutes. Move chicken to side of wok.

3 Add oil to center of wok. Add onion, zucchini and bell pepper; cook and stir 2 minutes. Add coconut milk, bean sauce, gingerroot and salt; cook and stir chicken and vegetables until sauce coats mixture, chicken is no longer pink in center and mixture is thoroughly heated. Sprinkle with toasted coconut.

1 SERVING: Calories 170; Total Fat 6g (Saturated Fat 3g; Trans Fat 0g); Cholesterol 55mg; Sodium 400mg; Total Carbohydrate 8g (Dietary Fiber 2g); Protein 20g **EXCHANGES:** 1 Vegetable, 2½ Lean Meat **CARBOHYDRATE CHOICES:** ½

instant success

Toasted coconut adds an exotic tropical flavor, but just 2 tablespoons contain 4 grams of fat. By limiting the amount of coconut you use and buying reduced-fat coconut milk, you can still enjoy the taste without excess fat and calories.

20 minutes or less

creamy chicken and vegetables with noodles

PREP TIME **20 MINUTES**   START TO FINISH **20 MINUTES**   **4 SERVINGS**

5 **cups medium egg noodles (10 oz)**

2 **cups frozen mixed vegetables (from 12-oz bag), thawed, drained**

6 **medium green onions, sliced (6 tablespoons)**

1 **container (8 oz) garden vegetable cream cheese spread**

1¼ **cups milk**

1½ **cups chopped deli rotisserie chicken (from 2-lb chicken)**

½ **teaspoon garlic salt**

¼ **teaspoon black pepper**

2 **tablespoons French-fried onions (from 2.8-oz can), if desired**

1 Cook and drain noodles as directed on package. Set aside.

2 Meanwhile, spray 12-inch skillet with cooking spray; heat over medium heat. Cook mixed vegetables and green onions in skillet about 4 minutes, stirring frequently, until vegetables are crisp-tender. Stir in cream cheese and milk until blended. Stir in chicken, garlic salt and pepper; cook until hot.

3 Stir in noodles; cook until hot. Sprinkle with French-fried onions.

1 SERVING: Calories 620; Total Fat 25g (Saturated Fat 13g; Trans Fat 0.5g); Cholesterol 155mg; Sodium 1130mg; Total Carbohydrate 65g (Dietary Fiber 6g); Protein 32g **EXCHANGES:** 3 Starch, 1 Other Carbohydrate, 1 Vegetable, 3 Medium-Fat Meat, 1½ Fat **CARBOHYDRATE CHOICES:** 4

instant success

Choose 2 cups of your family's favorite frozen vegetable to use in place of the mixed vegetables. Corn, peas and green beans would all be good choices. To quickly thaw the frozen vegetables, place them in a colander or strainer; rinse with warm water until thawed. Drain well.

20 minutes or less

fettuccine with chicken and vegetables

PREP TIME **20 MINUTES**   START TO FINISH **20 MINUTES**   **4 SERVINGS**

1 **package (9 oz) refrigerated fettuccine**

2 **cups fresh small broccoli florets**

½ **cup Italian dressing (not creamy)**

1 **lb uncooked chicken breast strips for stir-fry**

1 **medium red onion, cut into thin wedges**

¼ **teaspoon garlic-pepper blend**

½ **cup sliced drained roasted red bell peppers (from 7-oz jar)**

Shredded Parmesan cheese, if desired

1 Cook fettuccine and broccoli together as directed on fettuccine package. Drain; toss with 2 tablespoons of the dressing. Cover to keep warm.

2 Meanwhile, in 12-inch nonstick skillet, heat 2 tablespoons of the dressing over medium-high heat. Cook chicken, onion and garlic-pepper blend in dressing 4 to 6 minutes, stirring occasionally, until chicken is no longer pink in center.

3 Stir roasted peppers and remaining ¼ cup dressing into chicken mixture. Cook 2 to 3 minutes, stirring occasionally, until warm. Serve chicken mixture over fettuccine and broccoli. Serve with cheese.

1 SERVING: Calories 460; Total Fat 17g (Saturated Fat 2g; Trans Fat 0g); Cholesterol 75mg; Sodium 460mg; Total Carbohydrate 42g (Dietary Fiber 4g); Protein 34g **EXCHANGES:** 2 Starch, ½ Other Carbohydrate, 4 Very Lean Meat, 3 Fat **CARBOHYDRATE CHOICES:** 3

speed it up

Check out your grocer's meat case for the numerous types of raw meat and poultry that are precut for stir-fries or stew.

smothered chicken

PREP TIME **30 MINUTES**   START TO FINISH **30 MINUTES**   **4 SERVINGS**

2 tablespoons butter

1 medium onion, sliced
  (about 1 cup)

1 package (8 oz) sliced fresh
  mushrooms (about 3 cups)

2 teaspoons sugar

1 jar (12 oz) chicken gravy

1 tablespoon dry sherry,
  if desired

1 deli rotisserie chicken (2 lb),
  cut into serving pieces,
  skin removed if desired

1 tablespoon chopped
  fresh parsley

1 In 12-inch skillet, melt butter over medium heat. Cook onion and mushrooms in butter 8 to 10 minutes, stirring occasionally, until onions are tender and beginning to brown. Stir in sugar. Cook about 3 minutes, stirring occasionally, until vegetables are very brown.

2 Stir gravy and sherry into vegetables. Add chicken; spoon sauce over chicken. Cover; cook 5 to 10 minutes, turning chicken once, until thoroughly heated. Sprinkle with parsley.

1 SERVING: Calories 390; Total Fat 20g (Saturated Fat 7g; Trans Fat 0.5g); Cholesterol 125mg; Sodium 1150mg; Total Carbohydrate 13g (Dietary Fiber 2g); Protein 39g **EXCHANGES:** 1 Starch, 5 Lean Meat, 1 Fat **CARBOHYDRATE CHOICES:** 1

instant success

If the chicken is cold or cut into quarters, the cook time to heat it will be a bit longer.

20 minutes or less

honey-dijon turkey tenderloins with fresh asparagus

PREP TIME **20 MINUTES**   START TO FINISH **20 MINUTES**
4 SERVINGS (4 TURKEY SLICES PLUS 1 CUP VEGETABLES EACH)

1 package (20 oz) boneless turkey breast tenderloins, sliced ½ inch thick

1 teaspoon dried thyme leaves

¾ teaspoon garlic-pepper seasoning

2 tablespoons olive oil

1 cup chicken broth

2 tablespoon coarse-grain Dijon mustard

1 tablespoon honey

1 tablespoon cornstarch

1 lb fresh asparagus, cut into 2-inch pieces (3 cups)

1½ cups grape tomatoes, halved

1 Sprinkle turkey with thyme and the garlic-pepper seasoning. In 12-inch skillet, heat 1 tablespoon of the oil over medium-high heat. Cook turkey in oil 5 to 7 minutes, turning once, until lightly browned and juice of turkey is clear when center of thickest part is cut (at least 165°F). Remove from skillet; set aside.

2 In small bowl, combine broth, mustard, honey and cornstarch.

3 In same skillet, heat remaining 1 tablespoon oil over medium-high heat. Add asparagus to oil; cook 3 minutes, stirring frequently. Add cooked turkey and broth mixture. Cook and stir 1 minute or until sauce thickens. Add tomatoes; cook 1 minute longer, stirring constantly.

1 SERVING: Calories 290; Total Fat 9g (Saturated Fat 1.5g; Trans Fat 0g); Cholesterol 95mg; Sodium 590mg; Total Carbohydrate 14g (Dietary Fiber 3g); Protein 37g **EXCHANGES:** ½ Other Carbohydrate, 2 Vegetable, 2 Very Lean Meat, 2½ Lean Meat **CARBOHYDRATE CHOICES:** 1

make it a meal

For a fantastic, no-fuss meal, serve this colorful skillet dish with brown-and-serve breadsticks or rolls and clusters of grapes.

italian turkey sausage skillet with feta cheese

PREP TIME **30 MINUTES**   START TO FINISH **30 MINUTES**   **6 SERVINGS**

2 **cups penne pasta**

4 **links (4 oz each) hot Italian turkey sausage, casings removed**

1 **medium zucchini, sliced (2 cups)**

1 **medium red bell pepper, cut into 2-inch strips**

1 **can (14.5 oz) diced tomatoes with basil, garlic and oregano, undrained**

3 **tablespoons red wine vinegar**

1 **cup frozen whole-kernel corn**

1 **package (4 oz) crumbled tomato-basil feta cheese (1 cup)**

1 Cook and drain pasta as directed on package; cover to keep warm.

2 Meanwhile, spray 12-inch skillet with cooking spray. Heat over medium-high heat. Cook sausage in skillet 5 minutes, stirring occasionally and breaking up sausage with spoon. Add zucchini and bell pepper; cook about 4 minutes, stirring frequently, until sausage is no longer pink and vegetables are crisp-tender.

3 Stir in tomatoes, vinegar and corn. Cook about 5 minutes, stirring frequently, until heated through. Stir in cooked penne and cheese just before serving.

1 SERVING: Calories 360; Total Fat 10g (Saturated Fat 3g; Trans Fat 0g); Cholesterol 55mg; Sodium 990mg; Total Carbohydrate 47g (Dietary Fiber 4g); Protein 22g **EXCHANGES:** 1 Starch, 2 Other Carbohydrate, 1 Vegetable, 2 Lean Meat, ½ Medium-Fat Meat **CARBOHYDRATE CHOICES:** 3

instant success

To quickly remove the casing from the Italian sausage links, insert the tip of a paring knife under one end of the casing and slit open along the length of the sausage, being careful not to cut into the sausage. Pull the casing open and let the sausage fall into the skillet.

after-work chicken noodle soup

PREP TIME **30 MINUTES**   START TO FINISH **30 MINUTES**   **4 SERVINGS**

2 **cups cut-up rotisserie or other cooked chicken**

2 **medium stalks celery, chopped (1 cup)**

2 **medium carrots, sliced (1 cup)**

1 **medium onion, chopped (½ cup)**

1 **tablespoon chopped fresh parsley or 1 teaspoon parsley flakes**

1 **teaspoon dried thyme leaves**

¼ **teaspoon black pepper**

2 **cloves garlic, finely chopped**

7 **cups chicken broth (from two 32-oz cartons)**

1 **cup wide egg noodles (2 oz)**

1 In 3-quart saucepan, heat all ingredients except noodles to boiling. Stir in noodles. Heat to boiling; reduce heat.

2 Simmer uncovered 8 to 10 minutes, stirring occasionally, until noodles and vegetables are tender.

1 SERVING: Calories 260; Total Fat 8g (Saturated Fat 2g; Trans Fat 0g); Cholesterol 70mg; Sodium 2070mg; Total Carbohydrate 17g (Dietary Fiber 2g); Protein 30g **EXCHANGES:** 1 Starch, 4 Very Lean Meat, 1 Fat **CARBOHYDRATE CHOICES:** 1

speed it up

This recipe is already streamlined, but to make it a bit quicker, substitute ¼ to ½ teaspoon garlic powder for the chopped fresh garlic.

home-style chicken noodle bowl

PREP TIME **30 MINUTES**   START TO FINISH **30 MINUTES**   **6 SERVINGS**

   1   **package (12 oz) frozen home-style egg noodles**

3½   **cups chicken broth (from 32-oz carton)**

   4   **medium carrots, sliced diagonally into ½-inch pieces (1½ cups)**

   1   **medium onion (halved lengthwise), cut into thin wedges (½ cup)**

   1   **teaspoon garlic-pepper seasoning**

1½   **cups bite-size broccoli florets**

   1   **tablespoon cornstarch**

   2   **cups cut-up cooked chicken**

1 Cook and drain noodles as directed on package; cover to keep warm.

2 Meanwhile, in 3-quart saucepan, heat 2½ cups of the broth to boiling, Stir in carrots, onion and garlic-pepper seasoning. Reduce heat to medium; cover and cook 6 minutes. Stir in broccoli; cook 2 to 4 minutes longer or until vegetables are crisp-tender.

3 In small bowl, combine remaining 1 cup broth and the cornstarch; stir into vegetable mixture. Cook over medium heat, stirring constantly, until sauce thickens. Increase heat to high. Stir in cooked noodles and chicken. Cook, stirring constantly, until heated through.

1 SERVING: Calories 270; Total Fat 4.5g (Saturated Fat 1g; Trans Fat 0g); Cholesterol 100mg; Sodium 670mg; Total Carbohydrate 35g (Dietary Fiber 2g); Protein 22g **EXCHANGES:** 2 Starch, ½ Vegetable, 2 Very Lean Meat, ½ Fat **CARBOHYDRATE CHOICES:** 2

speed it up

Keep extra cooked chicken stored in your freezer to thaw and use for recipes like this one. If you prefer, you can also purchase a 2-pound rotisserie chicken and cut up what you need.

turkey-spaetzle soup

PREP TIME **25 MINUTES**   START TO FINISH **25 MINUTES**   **6 SERVINGS**

2   tablespoons vegetable oil

1   large onion, finely chopped
    (1 cup)

1   medium carrot, finely chopped
    (½ cup)

1   medium stalk celery,
    finely chopped (½ cup)

1   clove garlic, finely chopped

¼   cup all-purpose flour

1   tablespoon chopped fresh or
    2 teaspoons dried thyme leaves

¼   teaspoon black pepper

2   cups diced cooked turkey

6   cups chicken broth (from
    two 32-oz cartons)

1   bag (12 oz) frozen spaetzle

    Chopped fresh parsley,
    if desired

1 In 4-quart saucepan, heat oil over medium-high heat. Cook onion, carrot, celery and garlic in oil about 2 minutes, stirring frequently, until crisp-tender.

2 Gradually stir in flour, thyme and pepper; cook and stir about 1 minute. Stir in turkey and broth; heat to boiling.

3 Stir in spaetzle. Cook 2 to 3 minutes, stirring occasionally, until spaetzle are tender. Sprinkle with parsley.

1 SERVING: Calories 240; Total Fat 10g (Saturated Fat 2.5g; Trans Fat 0g); Cholesterol 70mg; Sodium 1180mg; Total Carbohydrate 17g (Dietary Fiber 2g); Protein 21g **EXCHANGES:** 1 Starch, 2½ Lean Meat, ½ Fat **CARBOHYDRATE CHOICES:** 1

instant success

If you prefer, substitute 3 cups frozen egg noodles (from a 16-ounce bag) for the spaetzle.

grilled chicken-citrus salad

PREP TIME **30 MINUTES**   START TO FINISH **30 MINUTES**   **4 SERVINGS**

⅔ cup citrus vinaigrette dressing

4 **boneless skinless chicken breasts (about 1¼ lb)**

1 **bag (10 oz) ready-to-eat romaine lettuce**

2 **unpeeled apples, cubed (about 2 cups)**

½ **cup coarsely chopped dried apricots**

2 **medium green onions, sliced (2 tablespoons)**

½ **cup chopped honey-roasted peanuts**

1 Heat gas or charcoal grill. Place 2 tablespoons of the dressing in small bowl. Brush all sides of chicken with the 2 tablespoons dressing.

2 In large bowl, toss lettuce, apples, apricots and onions; set aside.

3 Place chicken on grill. Cover grill; cook over medium heat 8 to 10 minutes, turning once, until juice of chicken is clear when center of thickest part is cut (at least 165°F).

4 Add remaining dressing to lettuce mixture; toss. On 4 plates, divide lettuce mixture. Cut chicken crosswise into slices; place on lettuce. Sprinkle with peanuts.

1 SERVING: Calories 550; Total Fat 31g (Saturated Fat 4g; Trans Fat 0g); Cholesterol 90mg; Sodium 510mg; Total Carbohydrate 30g (Dietary Fiber 6g); Protein 39g **EXCHANGES:** 1 Fruit, ½ Other Carbohydrate, 1 Vegetable, 5½ Very Lean Meat, 5½ Fat **CARBOHYDRATE CHOICES:** 2

instant success

With so many wonderful prewashed salad greens available, feel free to use your favorite mix for this recipe.

grilled sesame-ginger chicken

PREP TIME **25 MINUTES**   START TO FINISH **25 MINUTES**   **4 SERVINGS**

2 **tablespoons teriyaki sauce**

1 **tablespoon sesame seeds, toasted**

1 **teaspoon ground ginger**

4 **boneless skinless chicken breasts (about 1¼ lb)**

1 Brush grill rack with vegetable oil. Heat gas or charcoal grill. In small bowl, mix teriyaki sauce, sesame seeds and ginger.

2 Place chicken on grill. Cover grill; cook over medium heat 15 to 20 minutes, brushing frequently with sauce mixture and turning after 10 minutes, until juice of chicken is clear when center of thickest part is cut (at least 165°F). Discard any remaining sauce mixture.

1 SERVING: Calories 190; Total Fat 6g (Saturated Fat 1.5g; Trans Fat 0g); Cholesterol 85mg; Sodium 420mg; Total Carbohydrate 2g (Dietary Fiber 0g); Protein 32g **EXCHANGES:** 4½ Very Lean Meat, 1 Fat **CARBOHYDRATE CHOICES:** 0

instant success

To toast sesame seeds, cook in an ungreased heavy skillet over medium-low heat 5 to 7 minutes, stirring frequently until browning begins, then stirring constantly until golden brown.

turkey-cheddar-chipotle burgers

PREP TIME **25 MINUTES**   START TO FINISH **25 MINUTES**   **4 BURGERS**

1 **package (20 oz) ground turkey**

2 **chipotle chiles in adobo sauce (from 7-oz can), finely chopped**

3 **sticks (1 oz each) Cheddar cheese, cut into ½-inch pieces (½ cup)**

½ **teaspoon salt**

4 **slices Cheddar cheese**

4 **burger buns, split**

4 **leaves leaf lettuce, if desired**

¼ **cup chunky-style salsa**

1 Heat gas or charcoal grill. In large bowl, mix turkey, chiles, cheese pieces and salt. Shape mixture into 4 patties about ¾ inch thick.

2 Place patties on grill over medium heat. Cover grill; cook 13 to 15 minutes, turning once, until meat thermometer inserted in center of patties reads at least 165°F. Top each burger with 1 slice cheese. Cover grill; cook about 30 seconds longer or until cheese begins to melt.

3 On bun bottoms, place lettuce and burgers; top each with 1 tablespoon salsa. Cover with bun top.

1 BURGER: Calories 450; Total Fat 23g (Saturated Fat 9g; Trans Fat 1g); Cholesterol 115mg; Sodium 900mg; Total Carbohydrate 24g (Dietary Fiber 1g); Protein 38g **EXCHANGES:** 1½ Starch, 2 Lean Meat, 1½ Medium-Fat Meat, 1 High-Fat Meat **CARBOHYDRATE CHOICES:** 1½

make it a meal

Serve these tasty burgers with your favorite French fried potatoes and crunchy creamy coleslaw.

mediterranean chicken-vegetable kabobs

PREP TIME **30 MINUTES**   START TO FINISH **30 MINUTES**   **4 SERVINGS**

BASTING SAUCE

- ¼ **cup fresh lemon juice**
- 3 **tablespoons olive or vegetable oil**
- 2 **teaspoons chopped fresh rosemary leaves**
- ½ **teaspoon salt**
- ¼ **teaspoon black pepper**
- 4 **cloves garlic, finely chopped**

CHICKEN AND VEGETABLES

- 1 **lb boneless skinless chicken breasts, cut into 1½-inch pieces**
- 1 **medium red bell pepper, cut into 1-inch pieces**
- 1 **medium zucchini, cut into 1-inch pieces**
- 1 **medium red onion, cut into wedges**
- 1 **lb fresh asparagus spears, trimmed**
- ¼ **cup crumbled feta cheese (1 oz)**

1 Heat gas or charcoal grill. In small bowl, mix basting sauce ingredients.

2 On 4 (15-inch) metal skewers, alternately thread chicken and cut vegetables, leaving about ¼-inch space between each piece. Brush with basting sauce.

3 Place kabobs on grill over medium heat. Cover grill; cook 10 to 15 minutes, turning and brushing frequently with sauce, until chicken is no longer pink in center. Add asparagus to grill for last 5 minutes of cooking, turning occasionally, until crisp-tender. Discard any remaining basting sauce. Sprinkle cheese over kabobs. Serve with asparagus.

1 SERVING: Calories 320; Total Fat 16g (Saturated Fat 4g; Trans Fat 0g); Cholesterol 80mg; Sodium 470mg; Total Carbohydrate 13g (Dietary Fiber 4g); Protein 31g **EXCHANGES:** 3 Vegetable, 3½ Very Lean Meat, 3 Fat **CARBOHYDRATE CHOICES:** 1

instant success

If you have time, marinate the chicken before grilling. Mix basting sauce ingredients in shallow glass or plastic bowl; add chicken and stir to coat. Cover and refrigerate at least 30 minutes but no longer than 6 hours, stirring occasionally. After threading chicken, reserve marinade to brush on chicken and vegetables during grilling.

chicken with peppers and artichokes

PREP TIME **30 MINUTES**　START TO FINISH **30 MINUTES**　**4 SERVINGS**

1　jar (6 oz) ready-to-serve marinated artichoke hearts, drained, marinade reserved

⅓　cup dry white wine or chicken broth

4　boneless skinless chicken breasts (about 1¼ lb)

2　medium red bell peppers, cut lengthwise into quarters

4　medium green onions, sliced (¼ cup)

¼　teaspoon black pepper

1 Heat gas or charcoal grill. Set artichokes aside. In small bowl, mix reserved marinade and the wine; set half of the mixture aside. Brush chicken and bell peppers with remaining marinade mixture.

2 Place chicken on grill over medium heat. Cover grill; cook 5 minutes. Turn chicken; add bell peppers to grill. Cover grill; cook 10 to 15 minutes or until peppers are tender and juice of chicken is clear when center of thickest part is cut (at least 165°F).

3 In 1-quart saucepan, mix reserved marinade mixture, the artichokes, onions and pepper. Heat to boiling; boil and stir 1 minute. Serve with chicken and bell peppers.

1 SERVING: Calories 200; Total Fat 5g (Saturated Fat 1.5g; Trans Fat 0g); Cholesterol 70mg; Sodium 210mg; Total Carbohydrate 9g (Dietary Fiber 5g); Protein 27g **EXCHANGES:** 1½ Vegetable, 3½ Very Lean Meat, ½ Fat **CARBOHYDRATE CHOICES:** ½

instant success

When bell peppers are at their peak, choose from a variety of vibrant colors—red, orange, yellow and green.

crunchy cornmeal chicken with mango-peach salsa

PREP TIME **30 MINUTES**   START TO FINISH **30 MINUTES**   **4 SERVINGS**

SALSA

- **3** **medium peaches, peeled, chopped (1½ cups)**
- **1** **ripe large mango, pitted, peeled and chopped (1½ cups)**
- **1** **large tomato, seeded, chopped (1 cup)**
- **¼** **cup chopped fresh cilantro**
- **3** **tablespoons vegetable oil**
- **2** **tablespoons white vinegar**
- **¼** **teaspoon salt**

CHICKEN

- **½** **cup yellow cornmeal**
- **½** **teaspoon salt**
- **¼** **teaspoon black pepper**
- **4** **boneless skinless chicken breasts (about 1¼ lb)**
- **2** **tablespoons vegetable oil**

1 In large bowl, mix all salsa ingredients. Cover; refrigerate until serving.

2 In shallow dish, mix cornmeal, salt and pepper. Coat chicken with cornmeal mixture.

3 In 10-inch skillet, heat oil over medium-high heat. Cook chicken in oil 15 to 20 minutes, turning once, until juice of chicken is clear when center of thickest part is cut (at least 165°F). Serve with salsa.

1 SERVING: Calories 450; Total Fat 22g (Saturated Fat 4g; Trans Fat 0g); Cholesterol 85mg; Sodium 520mg; Total Carbohydrate 30g (Dietary Fiber 5g); Protein 34g **EXCHANGES:** 2 Fruit, 5 Lean Meat, 1 Fat **CARBOHYDRATE CHOICES:** 2

instant success

You may substitute 3 cups chopped frozen (thawed) sliced peaches for the fresh peaches. Also you could use jarred mango slices, well drained, instead of the fresh mango.

burger bash

Step out of the ketchup, mustard and pickle routine to create your own signature burgers. Choose from the selection below or get creative and whip up a burger of your own. Cook beef patties under the broiler, on the grill or in a skillet until a thermometer inserted in the center reads 160°F.

1 **Bavarian-Style Burgers:** Spread thin layer of hot sweet mustard on split onion buns. Top cooked ground beef patties with Emmentaler cheese slices after turning. Place on buns and top with fried or caramelized onions.

2 **Caprese Burgers:** Mix equal parts mayonnaise and refrigerated basil pesto and spread on split Italian rolls. Top cooked ground beef patties with thick slices of fresh mozzarella cheese and sliced tomatoes; sprinkle with coarse ground pepper.

3 **Chicago Burgers:** Sprinkle ground beef patties with celery salt before cooking. Place cooked patties on poppy seed buns; top with yellow mustard, sweet pickle relish, chopped onions, tomato wedges and jarred green sport peppers or banana pepper rings.

4 **Avocado BLT Burgers:** Spread thin layer of mayonnaise on buns. Top cooked ground beef patties or cooked chicken patties (cook until thermometer inserted in center reads 165°F) with sliced avocado, crisp-cooked bacon, lettuce leaves and tomato slices.

5 **Hawaiian Burgers:** Top cooked ground beef patties with mozzarella cheese slices after turning. Place on buns and top with smoky barbecue sauce and grilled pineapple slices.

6 **Pepper Jack–Jalapeño Burgers:** Spread thin layer of chipotle mayonnaise on buns. Top cooked ground beef patties with pepper Jack cheese slices after turning. Place on buns and top with well-drained sliced pickled jalapeño peppers.

7 **Tex-Mex Burgers:** Mix 1 pound ground beef with 1-ounce package of fajita seasoning mix and ¼ cup finely chopped onion; shape into patties. Cook as desired to correct temperature. Place on buns and top with guacamole and salsa.

8 **Reuben Burgers:** Spread toasted rye bread or buns with Thousand Island dressing. Top cooked ground beef patties or cooked turkey patties (cook until thermometer inserted in center reads 165°F) with sliced Swiss cheese. Place on bread slices or in buns; top with well-drained sauerkraut and additional dressing if desired.

9 *(no photo)* **Barbecue Burgers:** Fill toasted burger buns with creamy deli coleslaw, cooked ground beef patties, Monterey Jack cheese slices and barbecue sauce.

10 *(no photo)* **Blue Cheese and Tomato Burgers:** Spread crusty French rolls or kaiser buns with blue cheese dressing. Top with cooked ground beef patties, sliced tomato, shredded romaine and crumbled blue cheese.

beef+pork

beef tenderloin and mushrooms in garlic butter sauce

PREP TIME **30 MINUTES**   START TO FINISH **30 MINUTES**   **4 SERVINGS**

6 tablespoons cold butter

4 beef tenderloin steaks, 1½ inches thick (about 1¾ lb)

½ teaspoon salt

¼ teaspoon black pepper

1½ cups sliced baby portabella mushrooms (about 3.5 oz)

2 cloves garlic, finely chopped

¾ cup dry white wine or nonalcoholic wine

1 In 10-inch skillet, melt 1 tablespoon of the butter over medium-high heat. Sprinkle beef steaks with salt and pepper. Cook beef in butter 6 to 8 minutes, turning once, until deep brown. Reduce heat to low. Cover; cook 6 to 8 minutes (beef will be almost done and continue to cook while standing). Transfer beef to platter; cover to keep warm.

2 Increase heat to medium. Add 1 tablespoon of the remaining butter to skillet. Add mushrooms and garlic. Cook 3 to 4 minutes, stirring once or twice, until tender. Add wine. Cook 4 to 5 minutes, stirring occasionally, until reduced to about one-third and mixture is slightly thick. Remove from heat.

3 Beat remaining butter, 1 tablespoon at a time, into sauce with wire whisk just until melted. Serve mushrooms and sauce over beef.

1 SERVING: Calories 470; Total Fat 31g (Saturated Fat 16g; Trans Fat 1.5g); Cholesterol 130mg; Sodium 480mg; Total Carbohydrate 1g (Dietary Fiber 0g); Protein 47g **EXCHANGES:** 7 Lean Meat, 2 Fat **CARBOHYDRATE CHOICES:** 0

speed it up

Love it or hate it, but jarred chopped garlic is a handy-dandy little time-saver! Also, look for presliced mushrooms for a "chopping-free" meal.

beef + pork

adobo beef tacos with avocado salsa

PREP TIME **25 MINUTES**   START TO FINISH **25 MINUTES**   **4 SERVINGS (2 TACOS EACH)**

beef + pork

8   soft corn tortillas (6 inches)
1   lb extra-lean (at least 90%) ground beef
1   medium onion (halved lengthwise), cut into thin slices
½   cup chopped fresh cilantro
1   can (10 oz) diced tomatoes with green chiles, undrained
1   chipotle chile in adobo sauce, finely chopped (from 7-oz can)
1   medium lime
2   medium avocados, pitted, peeled and coarsely chopped

1 Heat 10-inch skillet over medium-high heat. Lightly spray both sides of one tortilla with cooking spray. Cook tortilla in skillet 10 to 15 seconds per side, using tongs to flip, until tortilla firms up slightly and just begins to get brown spots. Place on plate; cover with towel to keep warm. Repeat with remaining tortillas.

2 In same skillet, cook beef and half the onions over medium-high heat 8 to 10 minutes, stirring frequently, until beef is thoroughly cooked. Stir in ¼ cup of the cilantro, the tomatoes and chile. Heat to boiling; reduce heat. Simmer about 5 minutes, stirring occasionally.

3 Meanwhile, in medium bowl, grate lime zest; squeeze juice from lime into bowl. Add avocados, the remaining onion and ¼ cup cilantro to lime juice mixture; toss to combine.

4 Using slotted spoon, fill tortillas with ground beef mixture; top with avocado salsa.

1 SERVING: Calories 440; Total Fat 21g (Saturated Fat 5g; Trans Fat 0.5g); Cholesterol 70mg; Sodium 300mg; Total Carbohydrate 35g (Dietary Fiber 9g); Protein 27g **EXCHANGES:** 1½ Starch, ½ Fruit, ½ Vegetable, 2½ Very Lean Meat, ½ Lean Meat, 3½ Fat **CARBOHYDRATE CHOICES:** 2

speed it up

Because the amounts aren't critical to the success of this recipe, you don't need to measure the grated lime zest and juice from the lime. In general, you can expect to get 1½ to 3 teaspoons grated zest and 2 to 3 tablespoons juice from a medium lime.

mexican pasta skillet

PREP TIME **30 MINUTES**   START TO FINISH **30 MINUTES**   **6 SERVINGS**

beef+pork

1 lb extra-lean (at least 90%) ground beef

1 jar (16 oz) mild chunky-style salsa

1 cup tomato sauce (from 15-oz can)

1½ cups water

2 cups regular or multigrain elbow macaroni (about 8 oz)

1 cup frozen whole-kernel corn (from 12-oz bag)

½ cup shredded reduced-fat sharp Cheddar cheese (2 oz)

Sliced ripe olives, if desired

1 In 12-inch skillet, cook beef over medium-high heat 5 to 7 minutes, stirring occasionally, until thoroughly cooked; drain.

2 Stir in salsa, tomato sauce and water. Heat to boiling. Stir in macaroni and corn. Reduce heat. Cover; simmer 12 to 15 minutes, stirring occasionally, until macaroni is tender.

3 Sprinkle with cheese. Cover; let stand 1 to 2 minutes or until cheese is melted. Sprinkle each serving with olives.

1 SERVING: Calories 370; Total Fat 6g (Saturated Fat 2.5g; Trans Fat 0g); Cholesterol 45mg; Sodium 650mg; Total Carbohydrate 53g (Dietary Fiber 3g); Protein 25g **EXCHANGES:** 3½ Starch, 2 Lean Meat **CARBOHYDRATE CHOICES:** 3½

make it a meal

Toss a crisp green salad with your favorite low-fat dressing and serve it with this family-style skillet meal. Fresh fruit makes a perfect dessert.

orange-teriyaki beef with noodles

PREP TIME **20 MINUTES**   START TO FINISH **20 MINUTES**   **4 SERVINGS**

1	lb boneless beef top sirloin, trimmed of fat, cut into thin strips
1	can (14 oz) beef broth
¼	cup teriyaki stir-fry sauce
2	tablespoons orange marmalade
	Pinch ground red pepper (cayenne)
1½	cups frozen sugar snap peas (from 24-oz bag)
1½	cups thin egg noodles (3 oz)

1 Spray 12-inch skillet with cooking spray. Cook beef in skillet over medium-high heat 2 to 4 minutes, stirring occasionally, until brown. Remove beef from skillet; keep warm.

2 In same skillet, mix broth, stir-fry sauce, marmalade and red pepper. Heat to boiling. Stir in sugar snap peas and noodles; reduce heat to medium. Cover; cook about 5 minutes or until noodles are tender.

3 Stir in beef. Cook uncovered 2 to 3 minutes or until sauce is slightly thickened.

1 SERVING: Calories 270; Total Fat 4.5g (Saturated Fat 1.5g; Trans Fat 0g); Cholesterol 80mg; Sodium 1190mg; Total Carbohydrate 27g (Dietary Fiber 2g); Protein 29g **EXCHANGES:** 1 Starch, 2 Vegetable, 3 Very Lean Meat, ½ Fat **CARBOHYDRATE CHOICES:** 2

speed it up

For speedy prep, look for cut-up beef for stir-frying in the meat case at the grocery store. If you are cutting up beef yourself, freeze it for 20 to 30 minutes first for easy cutting.

20 minutes or less

italian steak sandwiches

PREP TIME **20 MINUTES**   START TO FINISH **20 MINUTES**   **4 SANDWICHES**

beef+pork

1   **tablespoon butter**

1   **medium onion, thinly sliced**

4   **beef cube steaks (about 1½ lb)**

½   **teaspoon salt**

¼   **teaspoon black pepper**

¼   **cup basil pesto**

4   **kaiser buns, split (toasted in oven if desired)**

4   **slices (about ¾ oz each) mozzarella cheese**

1   **medium tomato, thinly sliced**

1 In 12-inch nonstick skillet, melt butter over medium-high heat. Cook onion in butter 3 to 4 minutes, stirring frequently, until tender; push to side of skillet.

2 Add beef steaks to skillet; sprinkle with salt and pepper. Cook 5 to 8 minutes, turning once, for medium doneness (160°F).

3 Spread pesto on cut sides of buns. Layer steaks, cheese, onion and tomato in buns.

1 SANDWICH: Calories 600; Total Fat 29g (Saturated Fat 11g; Trans Fat 1.5g); Cholesterol 95mg; Sodium 880mg; Total Carbohydrate 32g (Dietary Fiber 2g); Protein 52g **EXCHANGES:** 2 Starch, 6½ Very Lean Meat, 5 Fat **CARBOHYDRATE CHOICES:** 2

instant success

Have you ever thought of putting that killer spinach dip you can buy from the deli or refrigerated case on a sandwich? Try it if you don't have the pesto on hand.

strip steaks with mango-peach salsa

PREP TIME **20 MINUTES**   START TO FINISH **20 MINUTES**   **4 SERVINGS**

- ¼ cup finely chopped red bell pepper
- 2 teaspoons finely chopped seeded jalapeño chiles
- 1 teaspoon finely chopped or grated gingerroot or ¼ teaspoon ground ginger
- ¼ cup peach preserves
- 1 tablespoon fresh lime juice
- 1 small mango, cut lengthwise in half, pitted and chopped (1 cup)
- 4 boneless beef top loin steaks (New York, Kansas City or strip steaks; 6 oz each)
- 1 to 2 teaspoons Caribbean jerk seasoning

1 In medium bowl, mix bell pepper, chiles and gingerroot. Stir in preserves, lime juice and mango.

2 Set oven control to broil. Sprinkle both sides of beef with jerk seasoning. Place on rack in broiler pan. Broil with tops 4 to 6 inches from heat 6 to 10 minutes, turning once, until desired doneness. Serve with salsa.

1 SERVING: Calories 360; Total Fat 12g (Saturated Fat 4.5g; Trans Fat 0.5g); Cholesterol 75mg; Sodium 130mg; Total Carbohydrate 24g (Dietary Fiber 1g); Protein 40g **EXCHANGES:** 1½ Other Carbohydrate, 5½ Very Lean Meat, 2 Fat **CARBOHYDRATE CHOICES:** 1½

instant success

Fresh mango will be slightly soft to the touch. Cut lengthwise into two pieces, cutting as close to the pit as possible. Make crisscross cuts ½ inch apart into mango flesh. Turn each mango half inside out and scrape off the pieces. Canned or jarred mangoes may be used instead; be sure to drain them well.

mini meat loaves

½   cup ketchup

2   tablespoons packed
    brown sugar

1   lb lean (at least 80%)
    ground beef

½   lb ground pork

½   cup Original Bisquick® mix

¼   teaspoon black pepper

1   small onion, finely chopped
    (¼ cup)

1   egg

1 Heat oven to 450°F. In small bowl, stir ketchup and brown sugar until mixed; reserve ¼ cup for topping. In large bowl, stir remaining ingredients and remaining ketchup mixture until well mixed.

2 Spray 13 × 9-inch pan with cooking spray. Place meat mixture in pan; pat into 12 × 4-inch rectangle. Cut lengthwise down center and then crosswise into sixths to form 12 loaves. Separate loaves, using spatula, so no edges are touching. Brush loaves with reserved ¼ cup ketchup mixture.

3 Bake 18 to 20 minutes or until loaves are no longer pink in center and meat thermometer inserted in center of loaves reads 160°F.

1 SERVING: Calories 300; Total Fat 16g (Saturated Fat 6g; Trans Fat 1g); Cholesterol 105mg; Sodium 430mg; Total Carbohydrate 16g (Dietary Fiber 0g); Protein 22g **EXCHANGES:** ½ Starch, ½ Other Carbohydrate, 3 Medium-Fat Meat **CARBOHYDRATE CHOICES:** 1

make it a meal

These cute little loaves bake much faster than a traditional whole loaf, plus you get more of that tangy crust. Stick with the "mini" theme by serving cooked baby-cut carrots. Mashed potatoes finish the meal.

curried pork-vegetable stir-fry

PREP TIME **30 MINUTES**   START TO FINISH **30 MINUTES**
4 SERVINGS (1¼ CUPS PORK MIXTURE AND ¾ CUP RICE EACH)

1	**cup regular long-grain white rice**
2¼	**cups water**
1	**lb pork tenderloin, cut in half lengthwise, then cut crosswise into thin slices**
½	**lb fresh green beans**
1	**medium red bell pepper, cut into 1-inch pieces**
1	**medium yellow summer squash, cut into ¼-inch slices**
1	**cup Korma curry sauce**
¼	**cup chopped fresh cilantro**

1 Cook rice in 2 cups of the water as directed on package.

2 Meanwhile, spray 12-inch skillet or wok with cooking spray. Heat over medium-high heat. Cook pork in skillet 5 to 6 minutes, stirring frequently, until pork is no longer pink in center. Remove pork and juices from skillet.

3 Spray same skillet with cooking spray; cook green beans 5 minutes, stirring constantly. Add bell pepper and squash; cook 2 minutes, stirring frequently. Add remaining ¼ cup water; cover and cook 2 minutes longer or until vegetables are crisp-tender. Add curry sauce and pork (with juices) to skillet. Cover and cook 2 to 3 minutes, stirring frequently, just until heated through.

4 Serve over cooked rice; sprinkle each serving with 1 tablespoon cilantro.

1 SERVING: Calories 460; Total Fat 15g (Saturated Fat 7g; Trans Fat 0g); Cholesterol 75mg; Sodium 85mg; Total Carbohydrate 52g (Dietary Fiber 4g); Protein 29g **EXCHANGES:** 2½ Starch, 2½ Vegetable, ½ Very Lean Meat, 2 Lean Meat, 1½ Fat **CARBOHYDRATE CHOICES:** 3½

easy add-on

Make a top-your-own curry bar. Offer tasty toppings to pass at the table such as chopped peanuts, sliced almonds, thinly sliced green onions or toasted coconut.

fettuccine with italian sausage and olive sauce

PREP TIME **30 MINUTES**   START TO FINISH **30 MINUTES**   **4 SERVINGS**

beef + pork

1 package (9 oz) refrigerated fettuccine

1 lb bulk Italian pork sausage

2 cans (14.5 oz each) diced tomatoes with basil, garlic and oregano, undrained

1 can (8 oz) tomato sauce

½ cup assorted small pitted olives

½ cup shredded Parmesan cheese (2 oz)

1 Cook and drain fettuccine as directed on package.

2 Meanwhile, in 12-inch skillet, cook sausage over medium-high heat 5 to 7 minutes, stirring occasionally, until no longer pink; drain if necessary.

3 Stir tomatoes, tomato sauce and olives into sausage. Reduce heat to low. Cover; cook 10 to 15 minutes, stirring occasionally, to blend flavors. Serve sauce over fettuccine. Sprinkle with cheese.

1 SERVING: Calories 610; Total Fat 29g (Saturated Fat 10g; Trans Fat 0g); Cholesterol 75mg; Sodium 2340mg; Total Carbohydrate 57g (Dietary Fiber 3g); Protein 32g **EXCHANGES:** 2½ Starch, 1 Other Carbohydrate, 1 Vegetable, 3 High-Fat Meat, ½ Fat **CARBOHYDRATE CHOICES:** 4

instant success

Hot Italian sausage is a definite option here and would go especially well with the flavor of the olives, but if you live on the "mild" side, by all means, use the mild sweet version!

ham and broccoli fettuccine

PREP TIME **10 MINUTES**   START TO FINISH **30 MINUTES**   **4 SERVINGS**

8 oz fettuccine

2 cups bite-size broccoli florets

2 cups cubed cooked ham (8 oz)

1 teaspoon garlic-pepper blend

2 tablespoons chopped fresh parsley

1½ cups chicken broth

1 tablespoon cornstarch

½ cup grated Parmesan cheese

1 In 5-quart Dutch oven or saucepan, cook pasta as directed on package, adding broccoli during last 5 minutes of cook time; drain and return to Dutch oven. Stir in ham, garlic-pepper blend and parsley.

2 In small bowl, combine broth and cornstarch; add to fettuccine mixture. Cook over medium heat about 4 minutes, tossing gently, until mixture is heated through and sauce thickens slightly. Stir in cheese.

1 SERVING: Calories 450; Total Fat 13g (Saturated Fat 5g; Trans Fat 0g); Cholesterol 85mg; Sodium 1870mg; Total Carbohydrate 52g (Dietary Fiber 6g); Protein 31g **EXCHANGES:** 3 Starch, 2 Vegetable, ½ Very Lean Meat, 2 Lean Meat, 1 Fat **CARBOHYDRATE CHOICES:** 3½

speed it up

To get dinner on the table even faster and with fewer dishes to clean up, purchase cubed ham at your grocery store from the refrigerated packaged meat aisle.

cajun smothered pork chops

PREP TIME **20 MINUTES**   START TO FINISH **20 MINUTES**   **4 SERVINGS**

4   **bone-in pork loin chops,
     ½ inch thick (about 1¾ lb)**

2   **teaspoons salt-free extra-spicy
     seasoning blend**

2   **teaspoons canola oil**

½   **medium onion, sliced**

1   **jalapeño chile, seeded,
     chopped**

1   **can (14.5 oz) diced tomatoes,
     undrained**

1 Sprinkle both sides of pork chops with seasoning blend. In 12-inch nonstick skillet, heat oil over medium-high heat. Add onion and jalapeño; cook about 2 minutes, stirring occasionally, until slightly tender. Push mixture to one side of skillet.

2 Add pork to other side of skillet. Cook about 3 minutes, turning once, until brown. Add tomatoes. Heat to boiling; reduce heat. Cover; cook 4 to 8 minutes or until pork is no longer pink in center and thermometer reads 145°F; let rest at least 3 minutes.

1 SERVING: Calories 270; Total Fat 13g (Saturated Fat 4g; Trans Fat 0g); Cholesterol 90mg; Sodium 190mg; Total Carbohydrate 6g (Dietary Fiber 1g); Protein 32g **EXCHANGES:** ½ Starch, 4 Lean Meat **CARBOHYDRATE CHOICES:** ½

make it a meal

Serve these delicious pork chops with hot cooked rice and whole green beans. Pecan pie is the perfect dessert.

crispy italian bread crumb–coated pork chops

PREP TIME **20 MINUTES**   START TO FINISH **20 MINUTES**   **4 SERVINGS**

1 cup Italian-style crispy panko bread crumbs

1 teaspoon grated lemon zest

2 teaspoons chopped fresh oregano leaves

1 egg

¼ cup all-purpose flour

4 boneless pork loin chops, ½ inch thick (4 oz each)

2 tablespoons olive or vegetable oil

1 In medium bowl, combine bread crumbs, lemon zest and oregano. In shallow bowl, beat egg with fork or whisk until blended. Place flour in shallow dish. Coat pork with flour; dip in egg, then coat with bread crumb mixture.

2 In 12-inch nonstick skillet, heat oil over medium-high heat. Cook pork in oil 5 minutes; turn. Cook about 3 minutes longer or until pork is no longer pink in center and meat thermometer reads 145°F; let rest at least 3 minutes.

1 SERVING: Calories 390; Total Fat 18g (Saturated Fat 5g; Trans Fat 0g); Cholesterol 125mg; Sodium 510mg; Total Carbohydrate 26g (Dietary Fiber 1g); Protein 30g **EXCHANGES:** 1½ Starch, 3½ Lean Meat, 1½ Fat **CARBOHYDRATE CHOICES:** 2

make it a meal

Serve these flavorful chops with a crisp green salad and crusty bread for an easy, satisfying dinner.

garlic-basil pork patties with herbed aioli

PREP TIME **25 MINUTES**   START TO FINISH **25 MINUTES**   **4 SERVINGS**

beef+pork

- 1 **package (3 oz) fresh basil leaves**
- 4 **small cloves garlic**
- ¼ **cup mayonnaise**
- ⅛ **teaspoon black pepper**
- 1 **teaspoon grated lemon zest**
- 1 **lb lean ground pork**
- ¼ **teaspoon lemon-pepper with herbs seasoning**

1 Finely chop basil with garlic. To make aioli, in small bowl, mix 2 teaspoons of the basil mixture with mayonnaise, pepper and lemon zest until blended. Cover and refrigerate while making pork patties.

2 In medium bowl, mix remaining basil mixture with pork and lemon-pepper seasoning; shape into 4 patties, about ½ inch thick.

3 Heat 10-inch nonstick skillet over medium heat. Cook patties in skillet 10 to 12 minutes, turning once, until no longer pink in center and thermometer reads 160°F. Serve patties topped with aioli.

1 SERVING: Calories 330; Total Fat 27g (Saturated Fat 7g; Trans Fat 0g); Cholesterol 75mg; Sodium 150mg; Total Carbohydrate 2g (Dietary Fiber 0g); Protein 21g **EXCHANGES:** ½ Vegetable, ½ Lean Meat, 2½ Medium-Fat Meat, 2½ Fat **CARBOHYDRATE CHOICES:** 0

speed it up

To quickly chop the basil and garlic, place both in a food processor. Cover; process, using quick on-and-off motions, until finely chopped.

teriyaki-pineapple pork sandwiches

PREP TIME **25 MINUTES**   START TO FINISH **25 MINUTES**
4 SERVINGS (1 SANDWICH AND 3 TABLESPOONS SAUCE EACH)

1   tablespoon vegetable oil

1   medium red bell pepper,
    cut into 2-inch strips

1   lb boneless pork loin chops,
    thinly sliced

1   medium onion (halved
    lengthwise), cut into thin
    wedges

1   teaspoon garlic-pepper blend

½   cup teriyaki sauce

1   can (8 oz) pineapple slices
    in juice, drained, reserving
    ⅓ cup juice

4   onion buns, split

1 In 12-inch nonstick skillet, heat oil over medium-high heat. Cook bell pepper in oil 3 to 4 minutes, stirring frequently, until crisp-tender. Remove from skillet; set aside.

2 In same skillet, cook pork, onion and garlic-pepper blend over medium-high heat 7 to 9 minutes, stirring occasionally, until pork is no longer pink in center. Stir in teriyaki sauce and reserved pineapple juice; cook about 2 minutes, stirring occasionally, until heated through.

3 Meanwhile, set oven control to broil. On cookie sheet, place buns, cut side up. Broil with tops 5 to 6 inches from heat 1 to 2 minutes or until lightly toasted.

4 Using slotted spoon, fill buns with pork mixture. Top with pineapple slices and bell pepper. Serve sandwiches with teriyaki-pineapple sauce from pan for dipping.

1 SERVING: Calories 390; Total Fat 14g (Saturated Fat 4g; Trans Fat 0g); Cholesterol 70mg; Sodium 1700mg; Total Carbohydrate 37g (Dietary Fiber 2g); Protein 30g **EXCHANGES:** 1 Starch, ½ Fruit, ½ Other Carbohydrate, 1 Vegetable, 2½ Lean Meat, 1 Medium-Fat Meat **CARBOHYDRATE CHOICES:** 2½

make it a meal

For a superfast supper, pick up coleslaw and cut-up fresh fruit from the grocery store salad bar to serve with these delicious sandwiches.

beef 'n' veggie soup with mozzarella

PREP TIME **25 MINUTES**   START TO FINISH **25 MINUTES**   **8 SERVINGS**

beef+pork

1 **lb lean (at least 80%) ground beef**

1 **large onion, chopped (1 cup)**

2 **cups frozen mixed vegetables (from 1-lb bag)**

1 **can (14.5 oz) diced tomatoes with green pepper, celery and onions (or other variety), undrained**

4 **cups water**

5 **teaspoons beef bouillon granules**

1½ **teaspoons Italian seasoning**

¼ **teaspoon black pepper**

1 **cup shredded mozzarella cheese (4 oz)**

1 In 4-quart Dutch oven, cook beef and onion over medium-high heat 5 to 7 minutes, stirring occasionally, until beef is brown and thoroughly cooked; drain.

2 Stir in remaining ingredients except cheese. Heat to boiling; reduce heat. Simmer uncovered 6 to 8 minutes, stirring occasionally, until vegetables are tender.

3 Sprinkle about 2 tablespoons cheese in each of 8 soup bowls; fill bowls with soup.

1 SERVING: Calories 200; Total Fat 9g (Saturated Fat 4.5g; Trans Fat 0g); Cholesterol 45mg; Sodium 790mg; Total Carbohydrate 13g (Dietary Fiber 3g); Protein 16g **EXCHANGES:** ½ Other Carbohydrate, 1 Vegetable, 2 Medium-Fat Meat **CARBOHYDRATE CHOICES:** 1

make it a meal

Add some hearty rustic sourdough or Italian rolls for dipping into the soup and a Caesar salad for chilly, crunchy goodness to finish the meal.

spicy angel hair pasta and meatball soup

PREP TIME **25 MINUTES**   START TO FINISH **25 MINUTES**   **6 SERVINGS**

1   tablespoon olive oil

1   medium onion, chopped (½ cup)

3   cans (14.5 oz each) diced tomatoes with Italian herbs, undrained

2   cans (14 oz each) chicken broth

1   tablespoon sriracha sauce

½   teaspoon garlic salt

4   oz angel hair (cappellini) pasta, broken into 2-inch pieces

24   frozen cooked meatballs (from 24-oz bag)

1 In 5-quart Dutch oven, heat oil over medium-high heat. Cook onion in oil about 3 minutes, stirring occasionally, until tender. Stir in tomatoes, broth, sriracha sauce and garlic salt. Heat to boiling, stirring occasionally.

2 Stir in pasta and meatballs. Heat to boiling; reduce heat. Cover and simmer about 6 minutes, stirring occasionally, until pasta is tender and meatballs are thoroughly heated.

1 SERVING: Calories 460; Total Fat 19g (Saturated Fat 6g; Trans Fat 1g); Cholesterol 120mg; Sodium 1810mg; Total Carbohydrate 41g (Dietary Fiber 4g); Protein 30g **EXCHANGES:** 2 Starch, ½ Other Carbohydrate, 2 Lean Meat, 1½ Medium-Fat Meat, 1 Fat **CARBOHYDRATE CHOICES:** 3

instant success

Sriracha is a hot chile sauce made from ground chiles, vinegar, garlic, sugar and salt. It's thicker and not quite as hot as hot sauces typically used for Buffalo wings. Look for it near the international ingredients at the grocery store or at Asian markets.

deli beef and bean tossed salad

PREP TIME **10 MINUTES** START TO FINISH **10 MINUTES** **6 SERVINGS**

1 **bag (10 oz) mixed salad greens**

1 **can (15 oz) three-bean salad, chilled, or 1 pint (2 cups) deli three-bean salad**

¼ **lb cooked deli roast beef, cut into julienne strips (¾ cup)**

1 **cup shredded Cheddar or Swiss cheese (4 oz)**

12 **cherry tomatoes, cut in half**

In large bowl, toss all ingredients to combine.

1 SERVING: Calories 160; Total Fat 7g (Saturated Fat 4g; Trans Fat 0g); Cholesterol 30mg; Sodium 600mg; Total Carbohydrate 14g (Dietary Fiber 3g); Protein 11g **EXCHANGES:** ½ Starch, 1½ Vegetable, 1 Medium-Fat Meat, ½ Fat **CARBOHYDRATE CHOICES:** 1

instant success

You can substitute deli or leftover cooked ham or turkey instead of the beef. Feel free to use reduced-fat cheese, if you prefer.

grilled steak and potato salad

PREP TIME **30 MINUTES**   START TO FINISH **30 MINUTES**   **4 SERVINGS**

¾ lb small red potatoes, cut in half

⅔ cup honey Dijon dressing and marinade

1 boneless beef top sirloin steak, ¾ inch thick (¾ lb)

¼ teaspoon salt

¼ teaspoon coarsely ground black pepper

4 cups bite-size pieces romaine lettuce

2 medium tomatoes, cut into thin wedges

½ cup thinly sliced red onion

1 Heat gas or charcoal grill. In 2- or 2½-quart saucepan, place potatoes; add enough water to cover potatoes. Heat to boiling; reduce heat to medium. Cook uncovered 5 to 8 minutes or just until potatoes are tender.

2 Drain potatoes; place in medium bowl. Add 2 tablespoons of the dressing; toss to coat. Place potatoes in grill basket (grill "wok") if desired. Brush beef steak with 1 tablespoon of the dressing; sprinkle with salt and pepper.

3 Place beef and potatoes on grill. Cover grill; cook over medium heat 8 to 15 minutes, turning once, until beef is desired doneness (145°F for medium-rare) and potatoes are golden brown. Cut beef into thin slices.

4 Among 4 plates, divide lettuce, tomatoes and onion. Top with beef and potatoes; drizzle with remaining dressing. Sprinkle with additional pepper if desired.

1 SERVING: Calories 360; Total Fat 20g (Saturated Fat 4g; Trans Fat 0g); Cholesterol 35mg; Sodium 440mg; Total Carbohydrate 25g (Dietary Fiber 4g); Protein 22g **EXCHANGES:** ½ Starch, 1 Other Carbohydrate, 1 Vegetable, 2½ Lean Meat, 2½ Fat **CARBOHYDRATE CHOICES:** 1½

easy add-on

You won't have to twist the arm of blue cheese lovers to agree to a generous sprinkle of crumbled blue or Gorgonzola cheese on top of their salads.

caesar salad with grilled steak

PREP TIME **30 MINUTES**   START TO FINISH **30 MINUTES**   **4 SERVINGS**

beef+pork

DRESSING

- ¼ cup olive or vegetable oil
- ¼ cup fat-free egg product
- 1 tablespoon fresh lemon juice
- 1 teaspoon Dijon mustard
- 1 teaspoon anchovy paste
- 1 large clove garlic, finely chopped

SALAD

- 1 boneless beef top sirloin steak, 1 inch thick (1 lb)
- 1 tablespoon freshly ground black pepper
- 1 bunch romaine lettuce, torn into bite-size pieces
- 1 cup garlic-flavored croutons
- ½ cup shredded Parmesan cheese (2 oz)

1 Heat gas or charcoal grill. In tightly covered container, shake all dressing ingredients until well blended. Refrigerate until serving time.

2 Sprinkle beef with pepper. Place on grill over medium heat. Cover grill; cook 15 to 18 minutes for medium doneness (160°F), turning once. Cut beef across grain into thin slices.

3 In large bowl, toss romaine, croutons, cheese and dressing. Top with beef slices. Serve with additional shredded Parmesan cheese if desired.

1 SERVING: Calories 440; Total Fat 24g (Saturated Fat 6g; Trans Fat 1g); Cholesterol 90mg; Sodium 560mg; Total Carbohydrate 14g (Dietary Fiber 4g); Protein 42g **EXCHANGES:** 3 Vegetable, 4½ Lean Meat, ½ High-Fat Meat, 1½ Fat **CARBOHYDRATE CHOICES:** 1

speed it up

Look for packaged romaine hearts in your produce section for less waste than your average bunch of romaine.

grilled hamburger steaks with roasted onions

PREP TIME **25 MINUTES**   START TO FINISH **25 MINUTES**   **4 SERVINGS**

4   **lean ground beef patties (4 to 6 oz each)**

2   **tablespoons steak sauce**

1   **package (1 oz) onion soup mix (from 2-oz box)**

2   **large Bermuda or other sweet onions, cut in half, then thinly sliced and separated (6 cups)**

2   **tablespoons packed brown sugar**

1   **tablespoon balsamic vinegar**

1 Heat gas or charcoal grill. Cut 2 (12 × 8-inch) sheets of heavy-duty foil; spray with cooking spray. Brush beef patties with steak sauce; sprinkle with half of the dry soup mix.

2 Place half of the onions on center of each foil sheet. Sprinkle with remaining soup mix, brown sugar and vinegar. Bring up 2 sides of foil so edges meet. Seal edges, making tight ½-inch fold; fold again, allowing space for circulation and expansion. Fold other sides to seal.

3 Place packets and beef patties on grill. Cover grill; cook over medium heat 10 to 15 minutes, turning patties and rotating packets a half turn once or twice, until meat thermometer inserted in center of patties reads 160°F. To serve onions, cut large X across top of each packet; carefully fold back foil to allow steam to escape. Serve onions with patties.

1 SERVING: Calories 320; Total Fat 13g (Saturated Fat 5g; Trans Fat 1g); Cholesterol 70mg; Sodium 790mg; Total Carbohydrate 30g (Dietary Fiber 4g); Protein 22g **EXCHANGES:** 1½ Starch, 1½ Vegetable, 2 Medium-Fat Meat, ½ Fat **CARBOHYDRATE CHOICES:** 2

make it a meal

Lightly grill some burger buns for added crunchiness. Throw some frozen fries in the oven before starting the recipe. You'll be chowing down in no time!

beef + pork

sirloin steaks with cilantro chimichurri

PREP TIME **25 MINUTES**   START TO FINISH **25 MINUTES**   **4 SERVINGS**

beef + pork

1 cup loosely packed fresh cilantro

1 small onion, cut into quarters

2 cloves garlic, cut in half

1 jalapeño chile, cut in half, seeded

2 teaspoons fresh lime juice

2 teaspoons vegetable oil

1¼ teaspoons salt

2 teaspoons ground cumin

½ teaspoon black pepper

4 beef sirloin steaks, 1 inch thick (about 1½ lb)

1 Heat gas or charcoal grill. In food processor, place cilantro, onion, garlic, chile, lime juice, oil and ¼ teaspoon of the salt. Cover; process until finely chopped. Blend in 2 to 3 teaspoons water to make sauce thinner, if desired. Transfer to small bowl; set aside until serving time.

2 In small bowl, combine cumin, pepper and remaining 1 teaspoon salt; rub evenly over steaks. Place steaks on grill over medium heat. Cover grill; cook 7 to 10 minutes for medium-rare (145°F), turning once halfway through cooking.

3 Serve 2 tablespoons chimichurri over each steak.

1 SERVING: Calories 290; Total Fat 9g (Saturated Fat 2.5g; Trans Fat 0g); Cholesterol 120mg; Sodium 800mg; Total Carbohydrate 3g (Dietary Fiber 0g); Protein 48g **EXCHANGES:** ½ Vegetable, 4½ Very Lean Meat, 2 Lean Meat **CARBOHYDRATE CHOICES:** 0

instant success

Substitute a serrano chile for the jalapeño, or add a pinch of ground red pepper (cayenne) if chiles are not available.

flank steak with smoky honey mustard sauce

PREP TIME **30 MINUTES**   START TO FINISH **30 MINUTES**   **6 SERVINGS**

SAUCE

- ¼ **cup honey mustard dressing**
- 1 **tablespoon frozen (thawed) orange juice concentrate**
- 1 **tablespoon water**
- 1 **clove garlic, finely chopped**
- 1 **chipotle chile in adobo sauce (from 7-oz can), finely chopped**

STEAK

- 1 **beef flank steak (about 1½ lb)**
- 6 **flour tortillas for burritos (8 inches; from 11-oz package), heated as directed on package**

1 Heat gas or charcoal grill. In small bowl, mix all sauce ingredients. Place 2 tablespoons in separate bowl to brush on steak. On both sides of beef, make cuts about ½ inch apart and ⅛ inch deep in diamond pattern. Brush the 2 tablespoons sauce on both sides of beef.

2 Place beef on grill over medium heat. Cover grill; cook 17 to 20 minutes, turning once, until beef reaches desired doneness (145°F for medium-rare).

3 Cut beef across grain into thin slices. Serve with tortillas and remaining sauce.

1 SERVING: Calories 360; Total Fat 16g (Saturated Fat 4.5g; Trans Fat 1.5g); Cholesterol 55mg; Sodium 460mg; Total Carbohydrate 22g (Dietary Fiber 0g); Protein 31g **EXCHANGES:** 1½ Starch, 4 Lean Meat, ½ Fat **CARBOHYDRATE CHOICES:** 1½

instant success

Chipotle chiles are dried, smoked jalapeños. They have wrinkled, dark brown skin and a smoky, sweet, almost chocolaty flavor. Canned chipotles in adobo sauce are spicy as well as smoky.

grilled cheesy mini meat loaves

PREP TIME **20 MINUTES**   START TO FINISH **20 MINUTES**   **4 SERVINGS**

1 **lb extra-lean (at least 90%) ground beef**

¼ **cup unseasoned dry bread crumbs**

3 **tablespoons ketchup**

1 **teaspoon onion salt**

½ **teaspoon black pepper**

1 **egg**

½ **cup shredded Cheddar cheese (2 oz)**

4 **slices center-cut bacon (about 3½ oz), cut crosswise in half**

1 Heat closed medium-size contact grill 5 minutes. Position drip tray to catch drippings.

2 Meanwhile, in large bowl, mix all ingredients except bacon. On work surface, pat beef mixture into 7-inch square. Cut into 4 (3½-inch) squares.

3 When grill is heated, place beef squares on grill; top each with 2 half-slices bacon. Close grill; cook 6 to 10 minutes or until meat thermometer inserted in center of loaves reads 160°F and bacon is browned.

1 SERVING: Calories 320; Total Fat 18g (Saturated Fat 8g; Trans Fat 0.5g); Cholesterol 140mg; Sodium 880mg; Total Carbohydrate 9g (Dietary Fiber 0g); Protein 30g **EXCHANGES:** ½ Starch, 3½ Medium-Fat Meat **CARBOHYDRATE CHOICES:** ½

instant success

Center-cut bacon has had the fatty ends cut off. You can use slices of regular bacon—just trim about ¾ inch off of each end. The half-strips should just cover the surface of each beef square.

grilled chili-rubbed pork tenderloin

PREP TIME **30 MINUTES**   START TO FINISH **30 MINUTES**   **4 SERVINGS**

2	teaspoons packed brown sugar
1½	teaspoons chili powder
1	teaspoon salt
1	teaspoon ground cumin
⅛	teaspoon ground red pepper (cayenne)
1	clove garlic, finely chopped
1	pork tenderloin (about 1 lb)
1	teaspoon vegetable oil

1 Heat gas or charcoal grill. In small bowl, mix all ingredients except pork and oil. Brush pork with oil. Rub and press spice mixture on all sides of pork.

2 Place pork on grill. Cover grill; cook over medium heat 17 to 20 minutes, turning several times, until meat thermometer inserted in center reads 145°F. Remove from grill. Cover pork; let rest at least 3 minutes. Cut pork into slices.

1 SERVING: Calories 170; Total Fat 6g (Saturated Fat 1.5g; Trans Fat 0g); Cholesterol 70mg; Sodium 650mg; Total Carbohydrate 3g (Dietary Fiber 0g); Protein 26g **EXCHANGES:** 3½ Very Lean Meat, 1 Fat **CARBOHYDRATE CHOICES:** 0

easy add-on

Imagine lively seasoned butter melting over this tender grilled pork! Just mix up a little extra of the seasoning rub mixture and stir it into softened butter. Pass it around to top the pork.

ginger pork with wasabi aioli

PREP TIME **30 MINUTES**   START TO FINISH **30 MINUTES**   **4 SERVINGS**

beef + pork

PORK

2 teaspoons ground ginger

½ teaspoon salt

½ teaspoon black pepper

1 pork tenderloin (about 1 lb)

1 teaspoon vegetable oil

AIOLI

¼ cup mayonnaise

2 teaspoons wasabi powder

1 clove garlic, finely chopped

1 Heat gas or charcoal grill. In small bowl, mix ginger, salt and pepper. Brush pork with oil; rub and press ginger mixture on all sides of pork.

2 Place pork on grill over medium heat. Cover grill; cook 17 to 20 minutes, turning several times, until meat thermometer inserted in center reads 145°F. Remove from grill. Cover pork; let rest at least 3 minutes.

3 Meanwhile, in small bowl, mix aioli ingredients. Cut pork into thin slices; serve with aioli.

1 SERVING: Calories 250; Total Fat 17g (Saturated Fat 3.5g; Trans Fat 0g); Cholesterol 55mg; Sodium 430mg; Total Carbohydrate 2g (Dietary Fiber 0g); Protein 22g **EXCHANGES:** 3 Lean Meat, 1½ Fat **CARBOHYDRATE CHOICES:** 0

instant success

To cook the pork evenly, tuck under any thin edge of tenderloin and secure with kitchen string; remove string before slicing.

pork kabobs

PREP TIME **30 MINUTES**   START TO FINISH **30 MINUTES**   **4 SERVINGS (2 KABOBS EACH)**

4   **boneless pork loin chops, ½ to ¾ inch thick (1 lb), trimmed of fat**

½   **teaspoon seasoned salt or pork seasoning**

2   **small zucchini, each cut into 8 pieces**

8   **medium mushrooms**

1   **medium red bell pepper, cut into 8 pieces**

½   **cup apricot preserves**

1   **tablespoon cider vinegar**

1 Heat gas or charcoal grill. Sprinkle both sides of pork chops with seasoned salt; cut each chop into 4 pieces.

2 On 8 (8-inch) metal skewers, alternately thread pork, zucchini, mushrooms and bell pepper. In small bowl, mix preserves and vinegar.

3 Place kabobs on grill over medium heat. Brush with half of preserves mixture. Cook uncovered 5 minutes. Turn kabobs; brush with remaining preserves mixture. Cook 5 to 7 minutes longer or until pork is no longer pink. If desired, serve over hot cooked rice.

1 SERVING: Calories 320; Total Fat 9g (Saturated Fat 3g; Trans Fat 0g); Cholesterol 70mg; Sodium 230mg; Total Carbohydrate 33g (Dietary Fiber 2g); Protein 26g **EXCHANGES:** 1½ Other Carbohydrate, 2½ Vegetable, 3 Lean Meat **CARBOHYDRATE CHOICES:** 2

instant success

Kabobs can be broiled instead of grilled. Set oven control to broil. Assemble kabobs as directed and place on broiler pan; brush with half of preserves mixture. Broil 4 to 6 inches from heat 10 to 12 minutes, turning once and brushing with remaining preserves mixture.

beef + pork

betty crocker quick & easy   173

grilled pork chops with peach salsa

PREP TIME **25 MINUTES**   START TO FINISH **25 MINUTES**   **4 SERVINGS**

3 ripe medium peaches, peeled, chopped (about 1½ cups)

¼ cup finely chopped red bell pepper

2 tablespoons finely chopped red onion

1 tablespoon chopped fresh cilantro

2 teaspoons packed brown sugar

2 teaspoons fresh lime juice

¼ teaspoon finely chopped serrano or jalapeño chile

4 bone-in pork loin chops, ½ inch thick (1 lb)

1 tablespoon chili powder

1 Heat gas or charcoal grill. In medium bowl, mix peaches, bell pepper, onion, cilantro, brown sugar, lime juice and chile.

2 Rub both sides of pork chops with chili powder. Place pork on grill over medium heat. Cover grill; cook 6 to 9 minutes, turning once, until pork is no longer pink and meat thermometer reads 145°F. Remove from grill, cover, and let rest for at least 3 minutes. Serve pork chops with salsa.

1 SERVING: Calories 240; Total Fat 9g (Saturated Fat 3g; Trans Fat 0g); Cholesterol 65mg; Sodium 60mg; Total Carbohydrate 15g (Dietary Fiber 2g); Protein 24g **EXCHANGES:** 1 Other Carbohydrate, 3½ Very Lean Meat, 1½ Fat **CARBOHYDRATE CHOICES:** 1

instant success

If you don't have ripe peaches available, substitute about 1½ cups chopped fresh mango or pineapple.

beef + pork

pork chops with maple-apple glaze

PREP TIME **20 MINUTES**   START TO FINISH **20 MINUTES**   **4 SERVINGS**

¼   cup maple syrup

¼   cup apple butter

½   teaspoon ground mustard

4   bone-in pork loin chops
     (½ to ¾ inch thick),
     trimmed of fat

½   teaspoon garlic-pepper blend

¼   teaspoon salt

1 Heat gas or charcoal grill. In 1-quart saucepan, mix syrup, apple butter and mustard. Cook over low heat about 1 minute, stirring occasionally, until well blended.

2 Sprinkle pork with garlic-pepper blend and salt; place on grill over medium heat. Brush with maple mixture. Cover grill; cook 10 to 12 minutes, turning and brushing with maple mixture 2 or 3 times, until pork is no longer pink and meat thermometer inserted in center reads 145°F. Remove from grill, cover, and let rest at least 3 minutes. Discard any remaining maple mixture.

1 SERVING: Calories 260; Total Fat 8g (Saturated Fat 3g; Trans Fat 0g); Cholesterol 65mg; Sodium 190mg; Total Carbohydrate 23g (Dietary Fiber 0g); Protein 23g **EXCHANGES:** 1 Starch, ½ Other Carbohydrate, 2½ Lean Meat **CARBOHYDRATE CHOICES:** 1½

beef + pork

instant success

You may use maple-flavored syrup instead of the real maple syrup.

toppers and sauces for fish

Mix up one of the following delicious combinations and serve with any cooked fish fillets, steaks or even with cooked shrimp. The sauces will be equally delicious whether your fish is broiled, grilled, fried or coated with crumbs and cooked in a skillet.

1 **Avocado-Kiwi Salsa:** Gently stir 1 cup avocado cubes, ½ cup peeled chopped kiwifruit, 3 tablespoons sliced green onions, 1 tablespoon finely chopped seeded jalapeño chile, 2 tablespoons lime juice, 2 tablespoons chopped fresh cilantro and ¼ teaspoon salt just until mixed.

2 **Honey-Pecan Sauce:** Stir 3 tablespoons honey, 2 tablespoons melted butter, 2 tablespoons chopped pecans (toasted if desired), 2 teaspoons fresh lemon juice and 1 teaspoon coarse-grained mustard until well mixed.

3 **Sweet Pea–Mint Pesto:** Place 1 cup cooked cold sweet peas, 2 tablespoons chopped fresh mint leaves, 1 garlic clove, ¼ teaspoon each coarse pepper and salt, and ¼ cup each olive oil and shredded Parmesan cheese in food processor. Process just until blended.

4 **Tomato-Basil Butter:** Mix ½ cup softened butter, 3 tablespoons tomato paste and 1 tablespoon chopped fresh basil until well blended.

5 *(no photo)* **Cocktail Dipping Sauce:** Stir 1 cup ketchup, 1 tablespoon prepared horseradish, 1 teaspoon Worcestershire sauce and 2 or 3 drops hot pepper sauce until smooth.

6 *(no photo)* **Dill and Sour Cream Sauce:** Stir ½ cup sour cream, 3 tablespoons mayonnaise and 1 tablespoon chopped fresh dill weed until well blended.

7 *(no photo)* **Herb Butter:** Beat ½ cup butter until fluffy. Beat in 1 finely chopped garlic clove, 2 tablespoons chopped fresh herbs (basil, chives, oregano, savory, tarragon or thyme) and 2 teaspoons fresh lemon juice.

8 *(no photo)* **Orange-Chipotle Sauce:** Stir ½ cup honey mustard dressing, 2 tablespoons frozen orange juice concentrate, 1 or 2 chopped chipotle chiles in adobo sauce and 1 tablespoon chopped fresh cilantro until blended.

9 *(no photo)* **Sesame-Ginger Sauce:** Stir 1 cup mayonnaise, 2 tablespoons teriyaki baste and glaze sauce, 2 tablespoons finely chopped green onions, 2 teaspoons honey, 2 teaspoons sesame seeds and 2 teaspoons grated fresh gingerroot until blended.

10 *(no photo)* **Tartar Sauce:** Stir 1 cup mayonnaise, 2 tablespoons pickle relish, 1 tablespoon chopped fresh parsley, 1 tablespoon drained chipped pimientos and 1 tablespoon finely chopped green onion until well blended.

fish+shellfish

basil salmon and julienne vegetables

PREP TIME **15 MINUTES**   START TO FINISH **25 MINUTES**   **4 SERVINGS**

1 tablespoon butter

1 bag (1 lb) frozen bell pepper and onion stir-fry

1 medium zucchini, cut into julienne (matchstick-size) strips

1½ lb salmon fillets, about ½ inch thick, cut into 4 serving pieces

2 tablespoons chopped fresh basil leaves

½ teaspoon seasoned salt

1 teaspoon lemon-pepper seasoning

¼ cup chicken broth

1 In 12-inch nonstick skillet, melt butter over medium heat. Add bell pepper mixture. Cook and stir 2 minutes. Stir in zucchini.

2 Place fish, skin side down, in skillet, pushing down into vegetables if necessary. Sprinkle fish and vegetables with basil, seasoned salt and lemon-pepper seasoning. Pour broth over fish and vegetables.

3 Cover; cook over medium-low heat 8 to 10 minutes or until fish flakes easily with fork. Remove fish and vegetables from skillet with slotted spoon.

1 SERVING: Calories 320; Total Fat 13g (Saturated Fat 4.5g; Trans Fat 0g); Cholesterol 120mg; Sodium 450mg; Total Carbohydrate 12g (Dietary Fiber 2g); Protein 38g **EXCHANGES:** ½ Other Carbohydrate, 1 Vegetable, 5 Lean Meat **CARBOHYDRATE CHOICES:** 1

speed it up

Make short work of cutting up the zucchini with this technique. Cut the whole zucchini crosswise into 2- to 3-inch sections. Then, stand a section on its end and cut it from top to bottom into ⅛-inch slices. Next, lay the slices flat, stack them, and cut the stack lengthwise into ⅛-inch matchstick-shaped pieces.

fish + shellfish

creamy salmon and tortellini

PREP TIME **15 MINUTES**   START TO FINISH **25 MINUTES**   **6 SERVINGS**

1   package (20 oz) refrigerated
     cheese-filled tortellini

1   bag (12 oz) frozen sweet peas

1   container (12 oz) chive-and-onion
     sour cream potato topper

½   cup milk

¼   teaspoon black pepper

2   cans (5 oz each) boneless
     skinless red salmon,
     well drained

¾   cup shredded Romano cheese

1 In 5-quart Dutch oven or saucepan, cook tortellini as directed on package, adding peas during last 2 minutes of cooking. Drain; keep warm.

2 In same Dutch oven, heat potato topper, milk and pepper over medium heat 2 minutes, stirring frequently. Add cooked tortellini and peas; gently toss to coat. Add salmon; gently fold into tortellini mixture just until heated through. Serve immediately, sprinkling each serving with 2 tablespoons cheese.

1 SERVING: Calories 560; Total Fat 23g (Saturated Fat 13g; Trans Fat 0g); Cholesterol 120mg; Sodium 980mg; Total Carbohydrate 57g (Dietary Fiber 4g); Protein 31g **EXCHANGES:** 3 Starch, ½ Other Carbohydrate, ½ Vegetable, 3 Lean Meat, 2½ Fat **CARBOHYDRATE CHOICES:** 4

make it a meal

For a complete meal, serve this one-pan dish with Caesar salad and warm breadsticks.

brown butter fish florentine

PREP TIME **25 MINUTES**   START TO FINISH **25 MINUTES**   **4 SERVINGS**

¼ **cup all-purpose flour**

1 **lb tilapia fillets, about ½ inch thick, cut into 4 serving pieces**

½ **teaspoon salt**

1 **teaspoon lemon-pepper seasoning**

¼ **cup butter (do not use margarine, spread or tub products)**

1 **bag (9 oz) washed fresh baby spinach leaves**

½ **red bell pepper, cut into very thin strips**

¼ **cup slivered almonds, toasted**

1. In shallow dish, place flour. Sprinkle fish with salt and lemon-pepper seasoning; dip in flour to coat.

2. In 12-inch nonstick skillet, heat butter over medium heat 3 to 4 minutes, stirring constantly, until light golden brown. Add fish. Cook 6 to 8 minutes, turning once, until outside is browned and fish flakes easily with fork. Transfer to plate; cover to keep warm.

3. Add spinach and bell pepper to butter in skillet. Cook 2 to 4 minutes, stirring frequently, until tender. On 4 dinner plates, spoon spinach mixture; top with fish. Sprinkle with almonds.

1 SERVING: Calories 300; Total Fat 17g (Saturated Fat 8g; Trans Fat 0.5g); Cholesterol 90mg; Sodium 610mg; Total Carbohydrate 11g (Dietary Fiber 3g); Protein 26g **EXCHANGES:** ½ Starch, 1 Vegetable, 3 Lean Meat, 1½ Fat **CARBOHYDRATE CHOICES:** 1

instant success

To toast the nuts, cook in an ungreased skillet over medium heat 5 to 7 minutes, stirring frequently until browning begins, then stirring constantly until golden brown. It's convenient to cook them in the skillet before you cook the fish.

orange and dill pan-seared tuna

PREP TIME **20 MINUTES**   START TO FINISH **20 MINUTES**   **4 SERVINGS**

1	**tablespoon butter**
1	**tablespoon olive or vegetable oil**
1½	**lb tuna, swordfish or other firm fish steaks, about ¾ inch thick, cut into 4 serving pieces**
1	**teaspoon peppered seasoned salt**
½	**cup thinly sliced red onion**
¾	**cup fresh orange juice**
1	**tablespoon chopped fresh or ¼ teaspoon dried dill weed**
1	**tablespoon butter or margarine**
1	**teaspoon grated orange zest, if desired**

1 In 10-inch nonstick skillet, heat 1 tablespoon butter and the oil over medium-high heat. Sprinkle both sides of fish with peppered seasoned salt. Add fish to skillet; cook about 1 minute on each side, until golden brown. Reduce heat to medium-low. Cook 3 to 4 minutes longer, turning once, until fish flakes easily with fork (tuna steaks will also be slightly pink in center). Remove fish from skillet; keep warm.

2 Add onion to skillet. Cook over medium heat 2 minutes, stirring occasionally. Stir in orange juice; cook 2 minutes. Stir in dill weed, 1 tablespoon butter and the orange zest. Cook 1 to 2 minutes or until slightly thickened. Serve sauce over fish.

1 SERVING: Calories 320; Total Fat 18g (Saturated Fat 7g; Trans Fat 0g); Cholesterol 115mg; Sodium 480mg; Total Carbohydrate 7g (Dietary Fiber 0g); Protein 33g **EXCHANGES:** ½ Other Carbohydrate, 4½ Very Lean Meat, 3 Fat **CARBOHYDRATE CHOICES:** ½

make it a meal

Fresh green beans or asparagus and lightly buttered new potatoes pair well with this citrus-flavored fish. For a stylish, easy garnish, use orange slices and dill sprigs.

fish + shellfish

tuna florentine

PREP TIME **25 MINUTES**   START TO FINISH **25 MINUTES**   **4 SERVINGS**

1   **box (8.4 oz) Betty Crocker Tuna Helper® creamy Parmesan**

2   **cups water**

1⅔ **cups milk**

3   **tablespoons butter**

¼   **teaspoon garlic powder**

1   **can (5 oz) tuna in water, drained**

1   **box (9 oz) frozen chopped spinach, thawed, squeezed to drain**

1   **cup cherry tomatoes, cut in half**

1   **tablespoon fresh lemon juice**

2   **tablespoons grated Parmesan cheese**

1 In 12-inch skillet, stir contents of pasta and sauce mix pouches (from Tuna Helper box), water, milk, butter and garlic powder. Heat to boiling over medium heat, stirring occasionally. Stir in tuna, spinach and tomatoes.

2 Reduce heat to medium-low. Cover; cook 13 to 15 minutes, stirring occasionally, until pasta is tender. Stir in lemon juice; sprinkle with cheese.

1 SERVING: Calories 420; Total Fat 15g (Saturated Fat 8g; Trans Fat 1.5g); Cholesterol 40mg; Sodium 1410mg; Total Carbohydrate 50g (Dietary Fiber 4g); Protein 21g **EXCHANGES:** 3 Starch, ½ Vegetable, 1½ Lean Meat, 2 Fat **CARBOHYDRATE CHOICES:** 3

instant success

Substitute a can of salmon or shrimp for the tuna. Make sure you drain it well before adding to the dish.

buttery tuna cakes

PREP TIME **25 MINUTES**   START TO FINISH **25 MINUTES**   **4 SERVINGS (2 TUNA CAKES EACH)**

36 **round buttery crackers**

2 **cans (5 oz each) chunk albacore (white) tuna in water, drained**

1 **egg**

½ **cup finely chopped red bell pepper**

¼ **cup finely chopped green onions (about 4)**

2 **tablespoons ranch dressing**

¼ **teaspoon black pepper**

2 **tablespoons butter**

1 In 1-gallon resealable food-storage plastic bag, place crackers. Seal bag; crush finely with rolling pin. In medium bowl, place 1 cup cracker crumbs (reserve remaining cracker crumbs). Add remaining ingredients except butter to cracker crumbs in bowl; mix gently.

2 Place reserved cracker crumbs in shallow bowl. Press tuna mixture into 8 patties, about ½ inch thick. Coat each patty with reserved cracker crumbs.

3 In 12-inch nonstick skillet, melt butter over medium-low heat. Cook tuna patties in butter 6 to 8 minutes, gently turning once, until golden brown and thoroughly heated.

1 SERVING: Calories 290; Total Fat 17g (Saturated Fat 6g; Trans Fat 0g); Cholesterol 35mg; Sodium 510mg; Total Carbohydrate 19g (Dietary Fiber 1g); Protein 16g **EXCHANGES:** 1½ Starch, 1½ Very Lean Meat, 3 Fat **CARBOHYDRATE CHOICES:** 1

easy add-on

These versatile cakes can be served alone, crab cake–style, or served in a burger bun sandwich-style. Top them with your favorite tartar sauce or seafood cocktail sauce.

tuna melt sandwiches

PREP TIME **15 MINUTES**   START TO FINISH **15 MINUTES**   **4 SANDWICHES**

4 slices whole-grain bread

2 cans (5 oz each) chunk albacore (white) tuna in water, drained

1 can (8 oz) crushed pineapple in juice, well drained (½ cup)

¼ cup light or regular mayonnaise

2 tablespoons finely chopped red onion

1 tablespoon finely chopped fresh or ½ teaspoon dried tarragon leaves

8 thin slices plum (Roma) tomatoes (1 large or 2 small)

4 slices (¾ oz each) Swiss cheese

1 Set oven control to broil. On cookie sheet, place bread. Broil with tops about 5 inches from heat 1 to 2 minutes per side or until lightly toasted.

2 In medium bowl, stir together remaining ingredients, except tomatoes and cheese, until well blended. Spread evenly on toasted bread slices; top each with 2 tomato slices and 1 cheese slice.

3 Broil 3 to 5 minutes or until cheese is melted and sandwiches are hot.

1 SANDWICH: Calories 300; Total Fat 13g (Saturated Fat 5g; Trans Fat 0g); Cholesterol 40mg; Sodium 460mg; Total Carbohydrate 23g (Dietary Fiber 3g); Protein 24g **EXCHANGES:** ½ Starch, 1 Other Carbohydrate, ½ Vegetable, 2½ Very Lean Meat, ½ High-Fat Meat, 1½ Fat **CARBOHYDRATE CHOICES:** 1½

instant success

To prevent corners and edges of the toasted bread slices from getting too dark when broiling, make sure to spread the tuna mixture to the edges.

linguine with tuna and tomatoes

PREP TIME **20 MINUTES**   START TO FINISH **20 MINUTES**   **4 SERVINGS**

8   oz linguine

½   cup crumbled feta cheese (2 oz)

2   cups cherry tomatoes, quartered, or coarsely chopped tomatoes

1   can (12 oz) solid white tuna in water, drained, flaked

2   tablespoons chopped fresh parsley

2   tablespoons olive, canola or soybean oil

1   clove garlic, finely chopped

¼   teaspoon salt

1 In 3-quart saucepan, cook linguine to desired doneness as directed on package. Drain; return to saucepan.

2 Reserve 2 tablespoons of the feta cheese for garnish. Add remaining feta cheese and remaining ingredients to linguine; toss to mix. Sprinkle with reserved feta cheese.

1 SERVING: Calories 440; Total Fat 12g (Saturated Fat 3.5g; Trans Fat 0g); Cholesterol 35mg; Sodium 780mg; Total Carbohydrate 54g (Dietary Fiber 4g); Protein 30g **EXCHANGES:** 3 Starch, 1 Vegetable, 2½ Lean Meat, ½ Fat **CARBOHYDRATE CHOICES:** 3½

instant success

Use extra-virgin olive oil in recipes such as this one where the oil is not heated. When extra-virgin olive oil is uncooked, its rich and fruity flavor really shines through.

herb-seasoned red snapper

PREP TIME **20 MINUTES**   START TO FINISH **20 MINUTES**   **4 SERVINGS**

2 **tablespoons grated Parmesan cheese**

1 **tablespoon finely chopped fresh parsley**

1 **tablespoon finely chopped fresh thyme leaves**

2 **teaspoons grated lemon zest**

1½ **lb red snapper fillets or other mild-flavored, medium-firm fish fillets, cut into 4 pieces**

½ **teaspoon salt**

2 **tablespoons vegetable oil**

2 **medium plum (Roma) tomatoes, thinly sliced**

1 In small bowl, stir together cheese, parsley, thyme and lemon zest.

2 Sprinkle fish with salt. In 12-inch nonstick skillet, heat oil over medium heat. Cook fish in oil, skin side up, 4 to 5 minutes or until golden brown. Turn gently; top with tomato slices. Cook 3 to 4 minutes longer or until fish flakes easily with fork. Sprinkle with cheese-herb mixture.

1 SERVING: Calories 230; Total Fat 10g (Saturated Fat 2g; Trans Fat 0g); Cholesterol 95mg; Sodium 490mg; Total Carbohydrate 2g (Dietary Fiber 0g); Protein 33g **EXCHANGES:** 4½ Very Lean Meat, 1½ Fat **CARBOHYDRATE CHOICES:** 0

instant success

Firm white fish such as rockfish or redfish may be substituted for the red snapper.

20 minutes or less

crab scampi with beer

PREP TIME **20 MINUTES**   START TO FINISH **20 MINUTES**   **4 SERVINGS**

10 oz spinach fettuccine
¼ cup butter
5 cloves garlic, finely chopped
1 cup Boston lager–style beer
1 package (8 oz) refrigerated flake-style imitation crabmeat
½ teaspoon salt
⅔ cup chopped fresh parsley
1 tablespoon grated lemon zest

1 In 5-quart Dutch oven or saucepan, cook fettuccine as directed on package. Drain and return to Dutch oven; keep warm.

2 Meanwhile, in 8-inch skillet, melt butter over medium heat. Cook garlic in butter 2 minutes, stirring frequently. Stir in beer; cook 2 minutes. Stir in crabmeat and salt, breaking up crabmeat into bite-size pieces with spoon. Cook 3 minutes, stirring frequently, until crabmeat is heated through. Pour over fettuccine; toss with parsley and lemon zest.

1 SERVING: Calories 420; Total Fat 15g (Saturated Fat 8g; Trans Fat 0g); Cholesterol 110mg; Sodium 1180mg; Total Carbohydrate 51g (Dietary Fiber 5g); Protein 18g **EXCHANGES:** 3½ Starch, 1 Very Lean Meat, 2½ Fat **CARBOHYDRATE CHOICES:** 3½

speed it up

With a food processor, you can make easy work of chopping the garlic and parsley for this recipe. Otherwise, pick up a jar of chopped garlic near the produce section at your grocery store.

scampi with fettuccine

PREP TIME **20 MINUTES** START TO FINISH **20 MINUTES** **4 SERVINGS**

8 oz fettuccine

2 **tablespoons olive or vegetable oil**

1½ **lb deveined peeled medium shrimp, thawed if frozen, tail shells removed**

2 **medium green onions, thinly sliced (2 tablespoons)**

2 **cloves garlic, finely chopped**

1 **tablespoon chopped fresh or ½ teaspoon dried basil leaves**

1 **tablespoon chopped fresh parsley**

2 **tablespoons fresh lemon juice**

¼ **teaspoon salt**

1 Cook and drain fettuccine as directed on package. Meanwhile, in 10-inch skillet, heat oil over medium heat. Cook remaining ingredients in oil 2 to 3 minutes, stirring frequently, until shrimp are pink; remove from heat.

2 Toss fettuccine with shrimp mixture in skillet.

1 SERVING: Calories 380; Total Fat 10g (Saturated Fat 1.5g; Trans Fat 0g); Cholesterol 290mg; Sodium 670mg; Total Carbohydrate 38g (Dietary Fiber 2g); Protein 33g **EXCHANGES:** 2½ Starch, 3½ Very Lean Meat, 1½ Fat **CARBOHYDRATE CHOICES:** 2½

speed it up

Peeling and deveining shrimp is time-consuming—and unnecessary! Luckily for us, somebody else has done this laborious task. Look for fresh or frozen shrimp that is already peeled and deveined.

fire-roasted tomato-shrimp veracruz

PREP TIME **15 MINUTES**   START TO FINISH **15 MINUTES**   **4 SERVINGS**

1   tablespoon olive oil

1   lb deveined peeled medium shrimp, thawed if frozen, tail shells removed if desired

¼   cup sliced green onions (4 medium)

1   fresh jalapeño or serrano chile, seeded, finely chopped

1   teaspoon grated orange zest

1   teaspoon chopped fresh or ½ teaspoon dried thyme leaves

1   can (14.5 oz) fire-roasted diced tomatoes, undrained

1 In 12-inch skillet, heat oil over medium-high heat. Add shrimp, green onions, chile, orange zest and thyme; cook 1 minute, stirring frequently.

2 Stir in tomatoes. Heat to boiling. Reduce heat; simmer uncovered about 5 minutes, stirring occasionally, until shrimp are pink and sauce is slightly thickened.

1 SERVING: Calories 140; Total Fat 4.5g (Saturated Fat 0.5g; Trans Fat 0g); Cholesterol 160mg; Sodium 320mg; Total Carbohydrate 6g (Dietary Fiber 1g); Protein 18g **EXCHANGES:** 1 Vegetable, 2½ Very Lean Meat, ½ Fat **CARBOHYDRATE CHOICES:** ½

make it a meal

Serve this saucy shrimp mixture over brown rice or whole wheat couscous. Then add steamed broccoli florets to finish the meal.

spicy lemon shrimp with basil mayonnaise

PREP TIME **20 MINUTES** START TO FINISH **20 MINUTES** **4 SERVINGS**

- 1 **tablespoon grated lemon zest**
- 3 **tablespoons fresh lemon juice**
- ¾ **teaspoon crushed red pepper flakes**
- ½ **teaspoon salt**
- 2 **cloves garlic, finely chopped**
- 2 **tablespoons olive or vegetable oil**
- 1 **lb deveined peeled large shrimp, thawed if frozen, tail shells removed**
- ½ **cup loosely packed fresh basil leaves**
- ½ **cup reduced-fat mayonnaise or salad dressing**

1 Set oven control to broil. In medium glass or plastic bowl, mix lemon zest, lemon juice, red pepper flakes, salt, garlic and 1 tablespoon of the oil. Add shrimp; toss to coat. In ungreased 15 × 10 × 1-inch pan, spread shrimp.

2 Broil shrimp with tops 2 to 3 inches from heat 3 to 5 minutes or until shrimp are pink.

3 In food processor, place basil and remaining 1 tablespoon oil. Cover; process until chopped. Add mayonnaise. Cover; process until smooth. Serve shrimp with mayonnaise.

1 SERVING: Calories 250; Total Fat 18g (Saturated Fat 2.5g; Trans Fat 0g); Cholesterol 170mg; Sodium 690mg; Total Carbohydrate 4g (Dietary Fiber 0g); Protein 18g **EXCHANGES:** 2½ Very Lean Meat, 3½ Fat **CARBOHYDRATE CHOICES:** 0

make it ahead

Using frozen shrimp is super convenient, but pat the thawed shrimp dry before adding to the oil mixture. Get to dinnertime even faster by making and refrigerating the basil mayonnaise up to a day before.

scallops with red bell pepper–cream sauce

PREP TIME **30 MINUTES**   START TO FINISH **30 MINUTES**   **4 SERVINGS**

1 cup roasted red bell pepper pieces, well drained (from a jar)

12 extra-large sea scallops (1 lb)

1 tablespoon lemon-pepper seasoning

2 tablespoons butter

1 large shallot, finely chopped (¼ cup)

1 tablespoon all-purpose flour

½ cup half-and-half

1 tablespoon chopped fresh chives

1 In food processor, place bell peppers. Cover; process 30 to 45 seconds, using quick on-and-off motions, until pureed; set aside.

2 Sprinkle tops of scallops with lemon-pepper seasoning. In 12-inch nonstick skillet, melt butter over medium heat. Cook scallops in butter 10 to 12 minutes, turning once about halfway through, until golden brown. Transfer from skillet to plate (do not discard pan juices); cover and keep warm.

3 In same skillet, cook shallot in reserved pan juices over medium heat 3 minutes, stirring occasionally, until tender. Sprinkle flour over shallot; stir until blended. Add pureed bell peppers and half-and-half; cook and stir 1 minute or until bubbly. Serve scallops with red bell pepper–cream sauce sprinkled with chives.

1 SERVING: Calories 190; Total Fat 10g (Saturated Fat 6g; Trans Fat 0g); Cholesterol 55mg; Sodium 560mg; Total Carbohydrate 9g (Dietary Fiber 1g); Protein 15g **EXCHANGES:** ½ Other Carbohydrate, ½ Vegetable, 2 Very Lean Meat, 2 Fat **CARBOHYDRATE CHOICES:** ½

instant success

Not all lemon-pepper seasoning blends are created equal. If your lemon-pepper doesn't contain salt, you may wish to check the seasoning level of the dish before serving to see if it needs a little salt.

angry tilapia rolls

PREP TIME **10 MINUTES**   START TO FINISH **30 MINUTES**   **4 SANDWICHES**

1 tablespoon Creole seasoning

2 teaspoons garlic-pepper blend

4 tilapia fillets or other mild-flavored, medium-firm fish fillets (3 to 4 oz each)

1 loaf (12 oz) baguette French bread (22 inches long), cut crosswise into 4 pieces

1 cup chopped hearts of romaine lettuce

2 oz Colby cheese, cut into 4 slices

¼ cup ranch dressing

1 to 2 teaspoons hot red pepper sauce

1 Heat oven to 375°F. Line cookie sheet with foil. In 1-gallon resealable food-storage plastic bag, combine Creole seasoning and garlic-pepper blend. Slice each fish fillet lengthwise into 3 or 4 strips, 1 to 1½ inches wide; place in bag. Seal bag; shake to coat.

2 Place fish on cookie sheet. Bake 12 to 15 minutes or until fish flakes easily with fork. Let stand 5 minutes.

3 Meanwhile, split each baguette by cutting lengthwise down through top to within ½ inch of bottom. For each sandwich, fill baguette with ¼ cup lettuce, 1 cheese slice and 2 to 3 pieces of fish; drizzle fish with 1 tablespoon dressing and ¼ to ½ teaspoon red pepper sauce.

1 SANDWICH: Calories 450; Total Fat 15g (Saturated Fat 4.5g; Trans Fat 0g); Cholesterol 65mg; Sodium 1520mg; Total Carbohydrate 50g (Dietary Fiber 2g); Protein 29g **EXCHANGES:** 2½ Starch, 1 Other Carbohydrate, 2½ Very Lean Meat, ½ High-Fat Meat, 1½ Fat **CARBOHYDRATE CHOICES:** 3

instant success

Have frozen tilapia fillets on hand? Be sure to thaw them in the refrigerator the night before you plan to make this recipe and pat them dry before using.

gremolata-topped sea bass

PREP TIME **5 MINUTES**   START TO FINISH **25 MINUTES**   **4 SERVINGS**

¼ cup Italian-style dry bread crumbs

¼ cup chopped fresh parsley

2 teaspoons grated lemon zest

1 tablespoon butter, melted

1 lb sea bass, mahi mahi or other medium-firm fish fillets, cut into 4 serving pieces

¼ teaspoon seasoned salt

1 tablespoon fresh lemon juice

1 Heat oven to 425°F. Line 13×9-inch pan with foil; spray foil with cooking spray. In small bowl, mix bread crumbs, parsley, lemon zest and butter.

2 Place fish in pan. Sprinkle with seasoned salt. Drizzle with lemon juice. Spoon crumb mixture over each piece; press lightly.

3 Bake 15 to 20 minutes or until fish flakes easily with fork.

1 SERVING: Calories 180; Total Fat 8g (Saturated Fat 3g; Trans Fat 0g); Cholesterol 65mg; Sodium 290mg; Total Carbohydrate 6g (Dietary Fiber 0g); Protein 23g **EXCHANGES:** ½ Starch, 3 Very Lean Meat, 1 Fat **CARBOHYDRATE CHOICES:** ½

instant success

It almost takes less time to assemble this dish than it takes to say "gremolata." This zesty citrus-flavored breading also makes a great topping for broiled lamb chops.

thai coconut-shrimp soup

PREP TIME **25 MINUTES**   START TO FINISH **25 MINUTES**   **6 SERVINGS**

1   **medium onion, chopped (½ cup)**

2   **cloves garlic, finely chopped**

2   **tablespoons red curry paste**

2   **cans (14 oz each) coconut milk (not cream of coconut)**

2   **cups chicken broth**

1   **tablespoon cornstarch**

1   **package (16 oz) frozen deveined peeled small (51 to 60 count), thawed, tail shells removed**

¼   **cup chopped fresh cilantro**

1 Spray 4-quart saucepan with cooking spray. Heat over medium heat. Cook onion in saucepan about 3 minutes, stirring frequently, until tender. Add garlic; cook and stir 1 minute. Stir in curry paste until melted. Stir in coconut milk; heat to boiling.

2 In small bowl, combine chicken broth and cornstarch; stir into coconut milk mixture. Stir in shrimp; reduce heat. Simmer about 2 minutes, stirring occasionally, just until shrimp turn pink. Garnish soup with cilantro.

1 SERVING: Calories 370; Total Fat 29g (Saturated Fat 25g; Trans Fat 0g); Cholesterol 110mg; Sodium 570mg; Total Carbohydrate 12g (Dietary Fiber 1g); Protein 15g **EXCHANGES:** 1 Starch, 1½ Very Lean Meat, 5½ Fat **CARBOHYDRATE CHOICES:** 1

instant success

Be sure to use regular coconut milk (not lite) for this recipe. The additional flavor and body from regular coconut milk really enhances the finished soup. Look for it near the other Asian ingredients at your grocery store.

fish + shellfish

honey-and-pecan-crusted cod salad

PREP TIME **5 MINUTES**   START TO FINISH **30 MINUTES**   **4 SERVINGS**

½ cup pecan halves

2¼ teaspoons Italian seasoning

4 cod fillets or other mild-flavored, medium-firm fish fillets (4 oz each)

2 tablespoons honey

¼ teaspoon salt

¼ cup olive oil

2 tablespoons balsamic vinegar

1 teaspoon honey

1 package (5 oz) mixed baby greens (about 8 cups)

12 cherry tomatoes, cut in half

1 Heat oven to 375°F. Line cookie sheet with foil. In food processor, place pecans and 2 teaspoons Italian seasoning. Cover; process, using quick on-and-off motions, until mixture is finely ground and resembles bread crumbs. Empty onto plate.

2 On one side of fillets, brush 2 tablespoons honey; press fillets, honey side down, into pecans. Place fillets, pecan side up, on cookie sheet. Bake 20 minutes or until fish flakes easily with fork. Let stand 5 minutes.

3 Meanwhile, in small bowl, mix remaining ¼ teaspoon Italian seasoning, salt, oil, vinegar and 1 teaspoon honey with whisk until blended.

4 In large bowl, place baby greens and tomatoes. Pour dressing over salad mixture; gently toss. Divide evenly among 4 plates. Top each salad with cod fillet.

1 SERVING: Calories 390; Total Fat 24g (Saturated Fat 3g; Trans Fat 0g); Cholesterol 60mg; Sodium 280mg; Total Carbohydrate 19g (Dietary Fiber 4g); Protein 24g **EXCHANGES:** 1 Other Carbohydrate, 1½ Vegetable, 3 Very Lean Meat, 4½ Fat **CARBOHYDRATE CHOICES:** 1

instant success

No food processor? Use a 1-gallon resealable food-storage plastic bag instead. Place the pecans and Italian seasoning in the bag and reseal. Cover the bag with a towel. With a rolling pin, smash the nuts until they're finely crushed and resemble bread crumbs.

grilled maple-dijon salmon and asparagus salad

PREP TIME **30 MINUTES**   START TO FINISH **30 MINUTES**   **4 SERVINGS**

DRESSING

- ⅓ **cup maple syrup**
- 2 **tablespoons Dijon mustard**
- 2 **tablespoons olive or vegetable oil**

SALAD

- 1 **lb asparagus spears**
- 1½ **lb salmon fillets, about ½ inch thick, cut into 4 serving pieces**
- 4 **cups fresh baby salad greens**
- 1 **cup shredded carrots (about 2 medium)**
- 2 **hard-cooked eggs, cut into 8 wedges**
- **Freshly ground black pepper, if desired**

1 Heat gas or charcoal grill. In small bowl, mix all dressing ingredients with whisk.

2 Snap off tough ends of asparagus spears. Brush fish with 1 tablespoon of the dressing. In 11×7-inch glass baking dish, toss asparagus and 1 tablespoon of the dressing. Place asparagus in grill basket (grill "wok").

3 Place grill basket and fish, skin side down, on grill. Cover grill; cook asparagus over medium heat 7 to 10 minutes, shaking grill basket or turning asparagus occasionally, until crisp-tender; cook fish 10 to 15 minutes or until fish flakes easily with fork.

4 Slide pancake turner between fish and skin to remove each piece from skin. Among 4 plates, divide salad greens, carrots and eggs. Top with fish and asparagus. Sprinkle with pepper. Serve with remaining dressing.

1 SERVING: Calories 420; Total Fat 19g (Saturated Fat 4g; Trans Fat 0g); Cholesterol 200mg; Sodium 370mg; Total Carbohydrate 27g (Dietary Fiber 3g); Protein 37g **EXCHANGES:** 1 Other Carbohydrate, 2 Vegetable, 4½ Lean Meat, 1 Fat **CARBOHYDRATE CHOICES:** 2

make it ahead

Too hot for a hot salad? Try it cold. Grill the salmon and asparagus, cook the eggs and make the dressing up to 1 day ahead of time. Cover and refrigerate until serving.

grilled lemon-salmon packets

PREP TIME **30 MINUTES**   START TO FINISH **30 MINUTES**   **4 SERVINGS**

1½ **lb salmon fillets, skin removed, cut into 4 serving pieces**

2 **tablespoons vegetable oil**

½ **teaspoon salt**

½ **teaspoon black pepper**

1 **medium lemon, cut into ⅛-inch slices (about 12)**

2 **tablespoons finely chopped fresh parsley**

1 Heat gas or charcoal grill. Cut 4 (18 × 12-inch) sheets of heavy-duty foil. Place 1 salmon piece on each sheet. Brush ½ tablespoon oil over both sides of each salmon piece. Sprinkle each with ⅛ teaspoon salt and ⅛ teaspoon pepper. Place about 3 lemon slices on each piece.

2 Bring up 2 sides of foil over salmon so edges meet. Seal edges, making tight ½-inch fold; fold again, allowing space for heat circulation and expansion. Fold other sides to seal.

3 Place packets on grill over medium-low heat. Cover grill; cook 13 to 16 minutes, rotating packets half turn after about 7 minutes, until salmon flakes easily with fork.

4 To serve, cut large X across top of each packet; carefully fold back foil to allow steam to escape. Sprinkle with parsley.

1 SERVING: Calories 310; Total Fat 17g (Saturated Fat 4g; Trans Fat 0g); Cholesterol 110mg; Sodium 400mg; Total Carbohydrate 3g (Dietary Fiber 1g); Protein 36g **EXCHANGES:** ½ Fruit, 5½ Very Lean Meat, 2 Fat **CARBOHYDRATE CHOICES:** 0

instant success

To store fresh herbs, wrap in slightly damp paper towels, place inside a resealable food-storage plastic bag and refrigerate. They will be ready to use when you need them.

fish + shellfish

grilled lemon-garlic halibut steaks

PREP TIME **20 MINUTES** START TO FINISH **30 MINUTES** **4 SERVINGS**

fish + shellfish

¼ cup fresh lemon juice
1 tablespoon olive or vegetable oil
¼ teaspoon salt
¼ teaspoon black pepper
2 cloves garlic, finely chopped
2 lb halibut or tuna steaks, about ¾ inch thick, cut into 4 serving pieces
¼ cup chopped fresh parsley
1 tablespoon grated lemon zest

1 Brush grill rack with vegetable oil. Heat gas or charcoal grill. In shallow glass or plastic dish or resealable food-storage plastic bag, mix lemon juice, oil, salt, pepper and garlic. Add fish; turn several times to coat. Cover dish or seal bag; refrigerate 10 minutes to marinate.

2 Remove fish from marinade; reserve marinade. Place fish on grill. Cover grill; cook over medium heat 10 to 15 minutes, turning once and brushing with marinade, until fish flakes easily with fork (tuna steaks will also be slightly pink in center). Discard any remaining marinade.

3 Sprinkle fish with parsley and lemon zest.

1 SERVING: Calories 240; Total Fat 6g (Saturated Fat 1g; Trans Fat 0g); Cholesterol 120mg; Sodium 340mg; Total Carbohydrate 2g (Dietary Fiber 0g); Protein 43g **EXCHANGES:** 6 Very Lean Meat, ½ Fat **CARBOHYDRATE CHOICES:** 0

easy add-on

Light and easy is the name of the game here. If you have a grill basket (grill "wok"), grill some snow peas for a crisp, refreshing side. Or cook them till crisp-tender in boiling water.

cajun halibut

PREP TIME **25 MINUTES**   START TO FINISH **25 MINUTES**   **4 SERVINGS**

RELISH

- **1 can (7 oz) whole-kernel corn, drained**
- **1 medium plum (Roma) tomato, chopped (⅓ cup)**
- **2 tablespoons chopped green onions**
- **1 tablespoon cider vinegar**
- **2 teaspoons honey**
- **¾ teaspoon dried oregano leaves**
- **¼ teaspoon ground red pepper (cayenne)**
- **¼ teaspoon salt**

FISH

- **4 halibut steaks (about 6 oz each)**
- **2 tablespoons Worcestershire sauce**
- **½ teaspoon coarsely ground black pepper**
- **¼ teaspoon dried oregano leaves**

1 Heat gas or charcoal grill. In small bowl, mix relish ingredients; set aside.

2 Brush halibut with Worcestershire sauce; sprinkle with black pepper and ¼ teaspoon oregano.

3 Place halibut on grill over medium heat. Cover grill; cook 10 to 15 minutes, turning once or twice, until fish flakes easily with fork. Serve with relish.

1 SERVING: Calories 220; Total Fat 2.5g (Saturated Fat 0.5g; Trans Fat 0g); Cholesterol 90mg; Sodium 520mg; Total Carbohydrate 15g (Dietary Fiber 1g); Protein 33g **EXCHANGES:** ½ Starch, ½ Other Carbohydrate, 4½ Very Lean Meat **CARBOHYDRATE CHOICES:** 1

instant success

Keep a spray bottle filled with water near the grill. Use it to douse any flare-ups that may occur.

tuna steaks with green onions and orange butter

PREP TIME **15 MINUTES**   START TO FINISH **20 MINUTES**   **4 SERVINGS**

¼ **cup butter, softened**

1 **tablespoon finely chopped green onion (1 medium)**

1 **teaspoon grated orange zest**

4 **teaspoons extra-virgin olive oil**

½ **teaspoon celery salt**

½ **teaspoon cracked black pepper**

4 **tuna steaks, 1 inch thick (about 1¼ lb)**

4 **green onions, trimmed**

1 Heat gas or charcoal grill. In small bowl, mix butter, 1 tablespoon chopped green onion and the orange zest; set aside.

2 In another small bowl, mix oil, celery salt and pepper. Brush oil mixture on both sides of tuna steaks and over whole green onions.

3 Place tuna on grill over medium heat. Cover grill; cook 8 to 10 minutes, turning once, until tuna flakes easily with fork and is slightly pink in center. Add onions to grill during last 5 minutes of grilling; turn occasionally. Cover tuna and let stand 5 minutes before serving. Serve tuna and onions with dollops of orange butter.

1 SERVING: Calories 330; Total Fat 23g (Saturated Fat 10g; Trans Fat 0g); Cholesterol 115mg; Sodium 350mg; Total Carbohydrate 2g (Dietary Fiber 0g); Protein 27g **EXCHANGES:** 4 Lean Meat, 2 Fat **CARBOHYDRATE CHOICES:** 0

easy add-on

Celery salt adds a nice flavor to the tuna, but plain salt may be substituted.

spicy shrimp fajitas

PREP TIME **30 MINUTES**   START TO FINISH **30 MINUTES**   **6 SERVINGS**

MARINADE

- 1 tablespoon fresh lime juice
- 1 tablespoon olive or vegetable oil
- 1 teaspoon salt
- 1 teaspoon chili powder
- 1 teaspoon ground cumin
- 2 cloves garlic, crushed
  Pinch ground red pepper (cayenne)

FAJITAS

- 2 lb deveined peeled medium shrimp, thawed if frozen, tail shells removed
- 2 medium red bell peppers, cut into strips (about 2 cups)
- 1 medium red onion, sliced (about 2 cups)
- 6 flour tortillas for burritos (8 inches; from 11.5-oz package)
- 1½ cups refrigerated guacamole (from 14-oz package)

1 Heat gas or charcoal grill. In 1-gallon resealable food-storage plastic bag, mix marinade ingredients. Add shrimp; seal bag and toss to coat. Set aside while grilling vegetables, turning bag once.

2 In medium bowl, place bell peppers and onion; spray with cooking spray. Place vegetables in grill basket (grill "wok"). Wrap tortillas in foil; set aside.

3 Place basket on grill rack over medium heat. Cover grill; cook 10 minutes, turning vegetables once.

4 Drain shrimp; discard marinade. Add shrimp to grill basket. Cover grill; cook 5 to 7 minutes longer, turning shrimp and vegetables once, until shrimp are pink. Place wrapped tortillas on grill. Cook 2 minutes, turning once, until warm.

5 On each tortilla, place shrimp, vegetables and guacamole; fold tortilla over filling.

1 SERVING: Calories 320; Total Fat 12g (Saturated Fat 2.5g; Trans Fat 1g); Cholesterol 175mg; Sodium 1140mg; Total Carbohydrate 29g (Dietary Fiber 3g); Protein 23g **EXCHANGES:** 2 Starch, 2½ Lean Meat, ½ Fat **CARBOHYDRATE CHOICES:** 2

instant success

Don't marinate the shrimp longer than 20 minutes or they'll start to cook in the marinade.

easy ways with tofu

Tofu is one of the most versatile, protein-rich foods for anyone who is looking for ways to eat more meatless meals. Soft silken tofu lends itself best to desserts and cream sauces, while firm and extra-firm tofu are best for stir-fries and baking. Here are some ideas for using tofu—there's even a dessert to sample!

1 **Asian Tofu Salad:** Cut extra-firm tofu into 1-inch cubes. Place cubes in skillet with 2 tablespoons Asian dressing and cook until golden brown, 10 to 12 minutes. Toss with mixed greens, shredded carrot, chopped cucumber, sliced green onions and additional Asian dressing. Sprinkle with sesame seeds.

2 **Chocolate-Banana Tofu Mousse:** In food processor, mix 1 package silken tofu and 2 ripe bananas until smooth. Fold 8 ounces melted semisweet chocolate into tofu mixture; add ¼ teaspoon vanilla. Spoon into 4 custard cups and chill 1 hour. Garnish with shaved chocolate.

3 **Fried Tofu with Peanut Sauce:** Cut extra-firm tofu into ½-inch cubes and coat with cornstarch. Cook in olive oil over medium heat about 5 minutes, until slightly browned. Stir in 2 tablespoons peanut sauce and serve over pasta. Sprinkle with green onions.

4 **Baked Sesame Tofu:** Cut extra-firm tofu into ½-inch slices; press with paper towel to remove moisture. Brush both sides with tamari sauce and sesame oil; let stand 10 minutes in baking dish. Bake at 325°F about 1 hour, turning halfway through, until firm to touch.

5 **Tofu Egg Salad:** Mix 2 tablespoons mayonnaise, 1 teaspoon Dijon mustard, 1 teaspoon fresh lemon juice, 1 tablespoon sweet pickle relish, 2 tablespoons diced celery and ¼ teaspoon dried dill weed. Fold in 8 ounces mashed firm tofu until blended. Sprinkle with paprika.

6 **Tofu Patties:** Mix 1 pound mashed extra-firm tofu (use fork), ½ cup panko bread crumbs, ½ cup ground walnuts, 1 tablespoon chopped green onion, ¼ teaspoon garlic salt and 1 to 2 tablespoons tamari sauce. Form into patties; cook in 1 tablespoon olive oil in skillet until brown and crisp on both sides.

7 **Tofu Spaghetti:** Freeze 1 package firm or extra-firm tofu, wrapped in plastic wrap, for 24 hours. Thaw; squeeze to remove moisture. Crumble tofu into tomato pasta sauce in saucepan. Simmer 15 minutes. Top with chopped fresh parsley and shredded Parmesan cheese. (Freezing, then thawing, makes tofu porous to absorb sauce for more flavor.)

8 **Veggie-Tofu Stir-Fry:** Cook and stir cubes of extra-firm tofu in mixture of 2 tablespoons each soy sauce, chili-garlic sauce and sweet chili sauce for 5 minutes. Add halved grape tomatoes and cook 2 to 3 minutes longer. Add 1 cup fresh baby spinach and cook just until wilted. Serve with cooked white rice.

meatless

tagliatelle pasta with asparagus and gorgonzola sauce

PREP TIME **25 MINUTES**   START TO FINISH **25 MINUTES**   **4 SERVINGS**

- 1 **lb asparagus**
- 8 **oz tagliatelle pasta or fettuccine**
- 2 **tablespoons olive or vegetable oil**
- 4 **medium green onions, sliced (¼ cup)**
- ¼ **cup chopped fresh parsley**
- 1 **clove garlic, finely chopped**
- 1 **cup crumbled Gorgonzola cheese (4 oz)**
- ½ **teaspoon freshly cracked black pepper**

1 Snap off tough ends of asparagus spears. Cut asparagus into 1-inch pieces. Cook pasta as directed on package, adding asparagus during last 5 minutes of cooking.

2 Meanwhile, in 12-inch skillet, heat oil over medium-high heat. Cook onions, parsley and garlic in oil about 5 minutes, stirring occasionally, until onions are tender. Reduce heat to medium.

3 Add pasta, asparagus and cheese to mixture in skillet. Cook about 3 minutes, tossing gently, until cheese is melted and pasta is evenly coated. Sprinkle with pepper.

1 SERVING: Calories 370; Total Fat 17g (Saturated Fat 7g; Trans Fat 0g); Cholesterol 70mg; Sodium 640mg; Total Carbohydrate 40g (Dietary Fiber 3g); Protein 15g **EXCHANGES:** 2 Starch, ½ Other Carbohydrate, 1 Vegetable, 1 High-Fat Meat, 1½ Fat **CARBOHYDRATE CHOICES:** 2½

instant success

Let your ingredients join forces! Adding vegetables to pasta water during the last minutes of cooking saves a major step (and saves you extra pans).

butternut squash risotto

PREP TIME **30 MINUTES**   START TO FINISH **30 MINUTES**   **4 SERVINGS**

4   cups vegetable broth

1   tablespoon olive oil

1   medium onion, chopped (½ cup)

2   cups ready-to-use cubed
    fresh butternut squash
    (from 16-oz package)

¼   cup dry white wine
    or vegetable broth

1   cup uncooked Arborio
    or regular long-grain rice

1   tablespoon garlic-and-herb
    seasoning

1   cup grated Parmesan cheese

1   bag (4½ oz) fresh baby spinach
    leaves

1 In 1½-quart saucepan, heat vegetable broth over medium-high heat just until simmering. Keep liquid at a simmer while preparing risotto.

2 Meanwhile, in 5-quart Dutch oven or saucepan, heat oil over medium-high heat. Cook onion and squash in oil 3 minutes, stirring occasionally, just until onion starts to soften. Add wine; cook until liquid is almost completely evaporated. Stir in rice and 1 teaspoon of the garlic-and-herb seasoning; cook 2 minutes, stirring frequently, until light brown.

3 Stir in 1 cup hot broth. Cook uncovered about 3 minutes, stirring frequently, until broth is absorbed; repeat with 2 more cups broth, adding 1 cup at a time. Stir in remaining 1 cup broth. Cook about 3 minutes longer, stirring frequently, until rice is just tender and mixture is creamy. Stir in remaining 2 teaspoons garlic-and-herb seasoning, the cheese and spinach just until spinach wilts. Serve immediately.

1 SERVING: Calories 380; Total Fat 11g (Saturated Fat 5g; Trans Fat 0g); Cholesterol 20mg; Sodium 1740mg; Total Carbohydrate 54g (Dietary Fiber 2g); Protein 15g **EXCHANGES:** 3 Starch, 2 Vegetable, ½ Lean Meat, 1½ Fat **CARBOHYDRATE CHOICES:** 3½

instant success

Many grocery and warehouse stores sell packages of ready-to-use cut-up butternut squash, which really saves on prep time. You can also use a 1¼ pound butternut squash, peeled, seeded and cubed, which will yield about 2 cups.

meatless

breaded tofu steaks with bell pepper–cucumber salad

PREP TIME **15 MINUTES**   START TO FINISH **30 MINUTES**   **6 SERVINGS**

TOFU STEAKS

- **1** **package (18 oz) extra-firm tofu, drained and sliced into 6 steaks, ½ inch thick**
- **¾** **cup Italian dressing**
- **2** **cups four-cheese Italian-herb baked crispy crackers, crushed (about 1 cup)**

BELL PEPPER–CUCUMBER SALAD

- **½** **cup whole-kernel sweet corn, drained (from 11-oz can)**
- **1** **red bell pepper, chopped (1 cup)**
- **1** **small cucumber, seeded, chopped (1 cup)**
- **2** **green onions, thinly sliced**

1 Heat oven to 425°F. On cookie sheet, place tofu between several layers of paper towels. Place a second cookie sheet, with about 5 lb weight, on top of paper towels. (Use 15- or 16-oz cans from pantry for weight.) Let tofu drain 5 minutes.

2 In 1-gallon resealable food-storage plastic bag, place tofu; pour ½ cup dressing over tofu in bag. Seal bag; gently rotate to coat. Let stand 5 minutes to marinate.

3 Meanwhile, in medium bowl, place all bell pepper–cucumber salad ingredients; toss with remaining ¼ cup dressing. Set aside.

4 Place cracker crumbs in shallow dish. Remove tofu from marinade (discard marinade); coat tofu in crumbs, pressing in lightly on both sides. Place on cookie sheet; bake 12 to 15 minutes or until golden brown.

5 To serve, place tofu on 6 plates; top each with about ⅓ cup bell pepper–cucumber salad.

1 SERVING: Calories 240; Total Fat 15g (Saturated Fat 1g; Trans Fat 0g); Cholesterol 0mg; Sodium 680mg; Total Carbohydrate 18g (Dietary Fiber 2g); Protein 8g **EXCHANGES:** ½ Starch, ½ Other Carbohydrate, ½ Vegetable, 1 Very Lean Meat, 3 Fat **CARBOHYDRATE CHOICES:** 1

instant success

Tofu comes in several firmness levels. For this recipe, look for extra-firm tofu; it's key for getting the "steak" consistency that you want for this dish.

salsa-rice burritos

PREP TIME **15 MINUTES**   START TO FINISH **20 MINUTES**   **8 BURRITOS**

1½ **cups salsa**

1½ **teaspoons chili powder**

1 **cup instant rice**

1 **can (15 oz) black beans, drained, rinsed**

1 **can (11 oz) whole-kernel corn with red and green peppers, undrained**

1½ **cups shredded Cheddar cheese (6 oz)**

8 **flour tortillas (8 inches)**

Additional salsa, if desired

1 In 10-inch skillet, heat 1½ cups salsa and the chili powder to boiling. Stir in rice; remove from heat. Cover; let stand 5 minutes.

2 Stir beans, corn and cheese into rice mixture.

3 Onto center of each tortilla, spoon about ½ cup rice mixture. Roll tortillas around filling; tuck ends under. Serve with additional salsa.

1 BURRITO: Calories 390; Total Fat 11g (Saturated Fat 5g; Trans Fat 0.5g); Cholesterol 20mg; Sodium 680mg; Total Carbohydrate 58g (Dietary Fiber 6g); Protein 16g **EXCHANGES:** 4 Starch, ½ Very Lean Meat, 1½ Fat **CARBOHYDRATE CHOICES:** 4

easy add-on

If you're a meat lover and have a few extra minutes, cook up some chorizo or ground beef and stir it into the rice mixture in step 2. Some brands of chorizo come in heat-and-serve links—even easier!

meatless

mozzarella-topped eggplant

PREP TIME **30 MINUTES**   START TO FINISH **30 MINUTES**   **4 SERVINGS**

1 medium eggplant (1½ lb), cut into 12 slices, ½ inch thick

3 tablespoons olive oil

⅔ cup Italian-style crispy panko bread crumbs

1½ teaspoons California-style garlic-pepper blend

¼ cup refrigerated sun-dried tomato pesto (from 6-oz container)

3 plum (Roma) tomatoes, coarsely chopped

8 oz fresh mozzarella cheese, cut into 12 slices

1 Place eggplant on work surface; brush both sides with oil. In shallow dish, stir together bread crumbs and garlic-pepper blend. Coat eggplant with bread crumb mixture (reserve any remaining bread crumb mixture); arrange in single layer on cookie sheet.

2 Set oven control to broil. Broil with tops 6 inches from heat 4 to 5 minutes or until light golden brown. Turn; sprinkle any reserved bread crumbs evenly over eggplant. Broil 4 to 5 minutes longer or until eggplant is tender and golden brown.

3 For each eggplant, spread with 1 teaspoon tomato-pesto and 1 tablespoon chopped tomato, and top with 1 cheese slice. Broil 2 to 3 minutes or just until cheese melts.

1 SERVING: Calories 440; Total Fat 28g (Saturated Fat 11g; Trans Fat 0g); Cholesterol 50mg; Sodium 1010mg; Total Carbohydrate 28g (Dietary Fiber 6g); Protein 18g **EXCHANGES:** 1 Starch, 3 Vegetable, 1½ High-Fat Meat, 3 Fat **CARBOHYDRATE CHOICES:** 2

instant success

To be sure your eggplant is tender but not overbrowned, broil at least 6 inches from the heating element. You can check to see if the eggplant is tender by piercing it with a fork.

meatless

italian parsley pesto ravioli

PREP TIME **25 MINUTES** START TO FINISH **25 MINUTES** **6 SERVINGS**

1 package (20 oz) refrigerated cheese-filled ravioli

2 cups fresh parsley

1 cup fresh basil leaves

1 clove garlic

1 cup grated Parmesan cheese

¾ cup chopped walnuts

¼ cup vegetable broth or olive oil

¼ cup reduced-sodium chicken broth

½ cup chopped drained roasted red bell peppers (from a jar)

1 Cook and drain ravioli as directed on package; return to pan. Cover to keep warm.

2 Meanwhile, in blender or food processor, place parsley, basil, garlic, ½ cup of the cheese, ¼ cup of the walnuts, the oil and broth. Cover and blend on medium speed about 3 minutes, stopping occasionally to scrape sides, until almost smooth.

3 Add basil mixture to cooked ravioli in pan; toss to coat. To serve, spoon onto serving platter; garnish with bell pepper and the remaining ½ cup walnuts. Serve with remaining ½ cup cheese.

1 SERVING: Calories 580; Total Fat 34g (Saturated Fat 11g; Trans Fat 0g); Cholesterol 65mg; Sodium 720mg; Total Carbohydrate 46g (Dietary Fiber 3g); Protein 22g **EXCHANGES:** 2½ Starch, 1 Vegetable, 1 Lean Meat, 1 Medium-Fat Meat, 5 Fat **CARBOHYDRATE CHOICES:** 3

instant success

To reduce the fat and trim the calories from this restaurant-worthy recipe, we replaced some of the oil typically found in pesto with broth.

penne with spicy sauce

PREP TIME **30 MINUTES**   START TO FINISH **30 MINUTES**   **6 SERVINGS**

1   **package (16 oz) penne pasta**

1   **can (28 oz) Italian-style peeled whole tomatoes, undrained**

2   **tablespoons olive or vegetable oil**

2   **cloves garlic, finely chopped**

1   **teaspoon crushed red pepper flakes**

2   **tablespoons chopped fresh parsley**

1   **tablespoon tomato paste (from 6-oz can)**

½   **cup freshly grated or shredded Parmesan cheese**

1 Cook and drain pasta as directed on package. Meanwhile, in food processor or blender, place tomatoes with juice. Cover; process until coarsely chopped.

2 In 12-inch skillet, heat oil over medium-high heat. Cook garlic, red pepper flakes and parsley in oil about 5 minutes, stirring frequently, until garlic just begins to turn golden. Stir in chopped tomatoes and tomato paste. Heat to boiling; reduce heat. Cover; simmer about 10 minutes, stirring occasionally, until slightly thickened.

3 Add pasta and ¼ cup of the cheese to mixture in skillet. Cook about 3 minutes, tossing gently, until pasta is evenly coated. Sprinkle with remaining ¼ cup cheese.

1 SERVING: Calories 400; Total Fat 9g (Saturated Fat 2.5g; Trans Fat 0g); Cholesterol 5mg; Sodium 640mg; Total Carbohydrate 66g (Dietary Fiber 6g); Protein 15g **EXCHANGES:** 4 Starch, 1 Vegetable, 1½ Fat **CARBOHYDRATE CHOICES:** 4½

easy add-on

Craving a meaty red sauce? Add sliced pepperoni with the chopped tomatoes in step 2 for a new taste sensation.

meatless

spaghetti with garbanzo beans

PREP TIME **25 MINUTES**   START TO FINISH **25 MINUTES**   **4 SERVINGS**

8 oz spaghetti

2 tablespoons olive oil

1 green bell pepper, chopped

3 cloves garlic, chopped

1 can (14.5 oz) fire-roasted crushed tomatoes, undrained

1 can (15 to 16 oz) garbanzo beans (chickpeas), drained

1 tablespoon Mediterranean herb seasoning

¼ cup shredded Parmesan cheese

1 Cook and drain spaghetti as directed on package except reserve ½ cup of the spaghetti cooking water. Cover spaghetti to keep warm.

2 Meanwhile, in 12-inch skillet, heat oil over medium heat. Cook bell pepper in oil 3 to 4 minutes, stirring occasionally, until tender. Add garlic; cook and stir 1 minute. Add tomatoes, garbanzo beans and Mediterranean-herb seasoning. Cook and stir until mixture begins to boil.

3 Add cooked spaghetti and ¼ cup reserved spaghetti water to tomato mixture in skillet. Cook, stirring frequently, until heated through. Add reserved spaghetti water, a few tablespoons at a time, until desired consistency. Garnish each serving with 1 tablespoon cheese.

1 SERVING: Calories 520; Total Fat 12g (Saturated Fat 2.5g; Trans Fat 0g); Cholesterol 0mg; Sodium 1190mg; Total Carbohydrate 81g (Dietary Fiber 10g); Protein 20g **EXCHANGES:** 3 Starch, 2 Other Carbohydrate, 1½ Vegetable, 1 Very Lean Meat, 2 Fat **CARBOHYDRATE CHOICES:** 5½

instant success

Pasta water has a lot of starch in it, making it a great way to add body to a pasta dish with sauce. Just save some of the pasta cooking water before draining the pasta. Then just before serving, add a little of it at a time until the pasta with sauce is the consistency you want.

spicy caprese pizza

PREP TIME **10 MINUTES**   START TO FINISH **25 MINUTES**   **4 SERVINGS**

1   **package (14 oz) prebaked original Italian pizza crust (12 inches)**

½   **cup roasted garlic-and-herb Italian tomato sauce (from 24-oz jar)**

½   **teaspoon crushed red pepper flakes**

1   **cup halved cherry tomatoes**

3   **sticks (1 oz each) string cheese, cut crosswise into ¼-inch slices**

½   **cup grated Parmesan cheese**

½   **cup thinly sliced fresh basil leaves**

2   **teaspoons olive oil**

1 Heat oven to 425°F. On cookie sheet, place pizza crust. Spread tomato sauce over crust, leaving a 1-inch border around edge. Sprinkle with pepper flakes. Arrange cherry tomatoes and string cheese on pizza. Sprinkle with Parmesan cheese.

2 Bake 15 minutes or until cheese is melted and just starting to bubble; remove from oven. Sprinkle basil evenly over pizza and drizzle with oil. Serve warm.

1 SERVING: Calories 440; Total Fat 16g (Saturated Fat 6g; Trans Fat 0g); Cholesterol 20mg; Sodium 900mg; Total Carbohydrate 54g (Dietary Fiber 3g); Protein 18g **EXCHANGES:** 2 Starch, 1½ Other Carbohydrate, 1 Vegetable, ½ Lean Meat, 1 Medium-Fat Meat, 1½ Fat **CARBOHYDRATE CHOICES:** 3½

instant success

Caprese salad lovers will enjoy having the flavors of fresh tomatoes, basil and mozzarella turned into a pizza. To get mozzarella distributed quickly, we sliced string cheese. It's much easier than having to grate fresh mozzarella for this pizza.

meatless

white bean and spinach pizza

PREP TIME **10 MINUTES**   START TO FINISH **30 MINUTES**   **8 SERVINGS**

2 cups water

½ cup sun-dried tomato halves (not oil-packed)

1 can (15 to 16 oz) great northern or navy beans, rinsed, drained

2 medium cloves garlic, finely chopped

1 package (14 oz) prebaked original Italian pizza crust (12 inches)

¼ teaspoon dried oregano leaves

1 cup firmly packed spinach leaves, shredded

½ cup shredded Colby–Monterey Jack cheese blend (2 oz)

1 Heat oven to 425°F. Heat water to boiling. In small bowl, pour enough boiling water over dried tomatoes to cover. Let stand 10 minutes; drain. Cut into thin strips; set aside.

2 In food processor, place beans and garlic. Cover; process until smooth.

3 Place pizza crust on ungreased cookie sheet. Spread beans over pizza crust. Sprinkle with oregano, tomatoes, spinach and cheese. Bake 8 to 10 minutes or until cheese is melted.

1 SERVING: Calories 240; Total Fat 6g (Saturated Fat 3g; Trans Fat 0g); Cholesterol 10mg; Sodium 370mg; Total Carbohydrate 36g (Dietary Fiber 4g); Protein 12g **EXCHANGES:** 2½ Starch, ½ Lean Meat, ½ Fat **CARBOHYDRATE CHOICES:** 2½

speed it up

In an extra bit of a hurry? Use a 7-ounce container of roasted garlic or regular hummus instead of processing the canned beans and garlic cloves in the food processor.

meatless

scrambled egg–grilled cheese sandwiches

PREP TIME **25 MINUTES**   START TO FINISH **25 MINUTES**   **4 SERVINGS (½ SANDWICH EACH)**

4   **eggs**

1   **tablespoon milk**

½   **teaspoon salt**

½   **teaspoon black pepper**

4   **slices sourdough bread (about ½ inch thick)**

2   **oz Havarti or dill Havarti cheese, cut into 4 slices**

4   **slices tomato**

1   **tablespoon butter**

1   In medium bowl, beat eggs, milk, salt and pepper thoroughly with fork or whisk until well mixed. Heat 10-inch nonstick skillet over medium heat. Pour egg mixture into skillet. As mixture begins to set at bottom and side, gently lift cooked portions with spatula so that thin, uncooked portion can flow to bottom. Avoid constant stirring. Cook 2 to 3 minutes or until eggs are thickened throughout but still moist.

2   To make sandwiches, divide eggs evenly between 2 bread slices. Layer each sandwich with 2 cheese slices and 2 tomato slices, and top with remaining bread slices. Spread ¾ teaspoon butter over each top slice of bread.

3   Wipe out skillet; heat over medium-high heat. Add sandwiches to skillet, buttered side down. Spread remaining butter over top slices of bread. Cook 4 to 5 minutes or until bottoms are golden brown. Turn; cook 4 to 5 minutes longer or until bottoms are golden brown and cheese is melted.

4   To serve, cut sandwiches in half; serve warm.

1 SERVING: Calories 260; Total Fat 14g (Saturated Fat 7g; Trans Fat 0g); Cholesterol 235mg; Sodium 690mg; Total Carbohydrate 20g (Dietary Fiber 1g); Protein 13g **EXCHANGES:** 1 Starch, ½ Other Carbohydrate, 1½ Medium-Fat Meat, 1 Fat **CARBOHYDRATE CHOICES:** 1

make it a meal

This recipe takes "grilled cheese" to a new level! For a satisfying and quick-to-fix weeknight meal, pair these comfort-food sandwiches with After-Work Chicken Noodle Soup (page 102).

meatless

garden vegetable wraps

PREP TIME **15 MINUTES**   START TO FINISH **15 MINUTES**   **4 SERVINGS**

½ cup cream cheese (about 4 oz), softened

4 flour tortillas (8 to 10 inches)

1 cup lightly packed spinach leaves

1 large tomato, thinly sliced

¾ cup shredded carrot

8 slices (1 oz each) Muenster or Monterey Jack cheese

1 small yellow bell pepper, chopped (½ cup)

1 Spread 2 tablespoons of the cream cheese over each tortilla. Top with spinach and tomato to within 1 inch of edge. Sprinkle with carrot. Top with cheese slices. Sprinkle with bell pepper.

2 Roll up tortillas tightly. Serve immediately, or wrap securely with plastic wrap and refrigerate up to 24 hours.

1 SERVING: Calories 480; Total Fat 30g (Saturated Fat 18g; Trans Fat 1g); Cholesterol 85mg; Sodium 670mg; Total Carbohydrate 31g (Dietary Fiber 3g); Protein 20g **EXCHANGES:** 2 Starch, 2 High-Fat Meat, 2 Fat **CARBOHYDRATE CHOICES:** 2

easy add-on

Customize your wrap by experimenting with flavored cream cheese, cooked frozen edamame, chopped fresh broccoli, sliced green onions or shredded zucchini. Or add your favorite cheeses and deli meats.

meatless

california veggie joes

PREP TIME **30 MINUTES**   START TO FINISH **30 MINUTES**   **6 SANDWICHES**

1 tablespoon olive oil

1 small onion, chopped (⅓ cup)

¾ cup bulgur

1½ cups water

1 can (15 oz) black beans with cumin and chili, drained

1 cup packed fresh cilantro

½ cup chili sauce

2 teaspoons soy sauce

6 whole wheat burger buns

6 leaves romaine lettuce, torn to fit buns if necessary

6 slices tomato

1 In 12-inch nonstick skillet, heat oil over medium-high heat. Cook and stir onion in oil 1 minute. Stir in bulgur and water; heat to boiling. Reduce heat, cover and simmer 8 to 10 minutes or until bulgur is tender and water is absorbed. Remove from heat; uncover and let stand 3 minutes.

2 In food processor, place bulgur mixture. Add beans, cilantro, chili sauce and soy sauce; cover and pulse 10 times or until chopped and blended. In same skillet, place bulgur-bean mixture. Cook over medium heat 3 to 4 minutes, stirring occasionally, until browned and thoroughly heated.

3 Split each bun in half to make a top and a bottom. Place 1 lettuce leaf on each bottom bun. For each sandwich, spoon about ½ cup bulgur mixture on lettuce; top with 1 tomato slice and cover with top of bun. Serve warm.

1 SANDWICH: Calories 290; Total Fat 4.5g (Saturated Fat 0.5g; Trans Fat 0g); Cholesterol 0mg; Sodium 780mg; Total Carbohydrate 49g (Dietary Fiber 12g); Protein 13g **EXCHANGES:** 2½ Starch, ½ Other Carbohydrate, ½ Vegetable, ½ Very Lean Meat, ½ Fat **CARBOHYDRATE CHOICES:** 3

make it a meal

Your family might think it's beef when they taste these savory sandwiches. For a no-fuss dinner, serve with deli pasta salad and fresh fruit.

meatless

veggie-stuffed portabellas

PREP TIME **30 MINUTES**   START TO FINISH **30 MINUTES**   **2 SERVINGS**

½ **lb fresh asparagus, trimmed, cut into 1-inch pieces**

¾ **cup frozen whole-kernel corn (from 12-oz bag)**

1 **cup soft bread crumbs (about 1½ slices bread)**

¼ **cup finely shredded Parmesan cheese (1 oz)**

2 **tablespoons chopped fresh chives**

2 **tablespoons vegetable broth**

½ **teaspoon salt**

⅛ **teaspoon black pepper**

4 **large portabella mushroom caps, stems removed**

1 **tablespoon olive oil**

1 Heat gas or charcoal grill. In 1-quart saucepan, heat ¼ cup water to boiling. Add asparagus. Cover; cook 4 minutes or until crisp-tender, adding corn during last 2 minutes of cooking time. Drain.

2 In medium bowl, mix asparagus, corn, bread crumbs, cheese, chives, broth, ¼ teaspoon of the salt and the pepper.

3 Brush mushroom caps with oil; sprinkle with remaining ¼ teaspoon salt. Place mushrooms, gill side down, on grill over medium heat. Cover grill; cook 5 minutes. Turn mushrooms over; mound about ½ cup vegetable mixture into each mushroom. Cover grill; cook 5 to 7 minutes longer or until stuffing is golden brown and cheese is melted.

1 SERVING: Calories 450; Total Fat 14g (Saturated Fat 4g; Trans Fat 0g); Cholesterol 10mg; Sodium 1280mg; Total Carbohydrate 62g (Dietary Fiber 8g); Protein 19g **EXCHANGES:** 1½ Starch, 1 Other Carbohydrate, 5 Vegetable, ½ Lean Meat, 2½ Fat **CARBOHYDRATE CHOICES:** 4

instant success

To make bread crumbs, tear a slice of bread into pieces and place in blender or food processor. Cover; process, using quick on-and-off motions, until crumbled.

meatless

teriyaki noodle bowls

PREP TIME **15 MINUTES**   START TO FINISH **15 MINUTES**   **4 SERVINGS**

1 tablespoon vegetable oil

3 green onions, cut into 1-inch pieces

2 cloves garlic, finely chopped

2 cups water

1 bag (1 lb) frozen bell pepper and onion stir-fry

2 packages (3 oz each) oriental-flavor or chicken-flavor ramen noodle soup mix

½ cup teriyaki sauce

¼ cup fresh orange juice

¼ cup honey-roasted peanuts, chopped

1 In 3-quart saucepan, heat oil over high heat. Cook and stir onions and garlic in oil 1 minute. Reduce heat to medium-high.

2 Add water, the pepper and onion stir-fry, noodles (gently broken into pieces), the contents of 1 seasoning packet (discard remaining packet or reserve for another use), teriyaki sauce and orange juice. Cover and cook about 8 minutes, stirring once or twice to separate noodles, until vegetables are crisp-tender. Serve in bowls; sprinkle with peanuts.

1 SERVING: Calories 290; Total Fat 13g (Saturated Fat 3g; Trans Fat 1.5g); Cholesterol 0mg; Sodium 1850mg; Total Carbohydrate 34g (Dietary Fiber 3g); Protein 9g **EXCHANGES:** 1½ Starch, 2 Vegetable, 2½ Fat **CARBOHYDRATE CHOICES:** 2

instant success

Be sure to use teriyaki sauce and not teriyaki marinade or baste-and-glaze for this recipe. The marinade and baste-and-glaze both have a much higher concentration of flavor and would be too strong.

meatless

tortilla green chili

PREP TIME **15 MINUTES**   START TO FINISH **15 MINUTES**   **4 SERVINGS**

1   **can (15 oz) black beans with cumin and chili, undrained**

1   **can (14.5 oz) diced tomatoes with green chiles, undrained**

1   **bag (12 oz) frozen whole-kernel corn**

1   **jar (16 oz) mild green tomatillo salsa**

½   **cup coarsely crushed tortilla chips (about 1 oz)**

1   **avocado, pitted, peeled and cubed**

1   **lime, sliced, slices cut into quarters**

¼   **cup sour cream**

    Additional tortilla chips, if desired

1 In 4-quart saucepan, heat beans, tomatoes, corn, salsa and tortilla chips to boiling; reduce heat to medium.

2 Cover and simmer 5 to 10 minutes, stirring occasionally, until slightly thickened. Ladle chili into 4 bowls; top each with avocado, lime, sour cream and, if desired, additional tortilla chips.

1 SERVING: Calories 390; Total Fat 13g (Saturated Fat 3g; Trans Fat 0g); Cholesterol 10mg; Sodium 940mg; Total Carbohydrate 56g (Dietary Fiber 14g); Protein 12g **EXCHANGES:** 2 Starch, ½ Fruit, ½ Other Carbohydrate, 1½ Vegetable, ½ Very Lean Meat, 2½ Fat **CARBOHYDRATE CHOICES:** 4

instant success

Crushed tortilla chips in chili? They're a surprise ingredient that adds flavor and thickness to the chili while cutting down on the number of ingredients and reducing the prep time. Crush them quickly in a 1-quart resealable food-storage plastic bag with a rolling pin.

meatless

easy italian white bean soup

PREP TIME **30 MINUTES**   START TO FINISH **30 MINUTES**   **4 SERVINGS**

2 cans (15 oz each) cannellini
  beans, rinsed, drained

2 teaspoons olive or vegetable oil

2 medium carrots, chopped
  (1 cup)

2 medium stalks celery,
  thinly sliced (1 cup)

¼ cup chopped onion

1 clove garlic, finely chopped

3 cups vegetable or chicken broth

1 teaspoon dried basil leaves

⅛ teaspoon black pepper

1 Mash ½ cup of the drained beans; leave the rest whole. In 3-quart saucepan, heat oil over medium-high heat. Cook carrots, celery, onion and garlic in oil 3 to 4 minutes, stirring frequently, until vegetables are crisp-tender.

2 Stir in broth, basil, pepper, mashed beans and remaining whole beans. Heat to boiling; reduce heat. Simmer uncovered 10 to 12 minutes, stirring occasionally, until vegetables are tender.

1 SERVING : Calories 280; Total Fat 3g (Saturated Fat 0g; Trans Fat 0g); Cholesterol 0mg; Sodium 1240mg; Total Carbohydrate 47g (Dietary Fiber 11g); Protein 16g **EXCHANGES:** 2 Starch, 3 Vegetable, ½ Very Lean Meat, ½ Fat **CARBOHYDRATE CHOICES:** 3

speed it up

Use 1 cup of purchased shredded carrots in place of the chopped carrots. Look for them with the precut vegetables in the grocery store's produce section.

meatless

italian tomato soup with pesto-cheese toasts

PREP TIME **15 MINUTES**   START TO FINISH **15 MINUTES**   **4 SERVINGS**

1 cup water

2 cans (14 oz each) diced tomatoes with Italian herbs, undrained

1 can (11.5 oz) tomato juice

4 slices rosemary, Italian or French bread, ½ inch thick

2 tablespoons basil pesto

2 tablespoons shredded Parmesan cheese

1 In 3-quart saucepan, heat water, tomatoes and tomato juice to boiling.

2 Set oven control to broil. Place bread on cookie sheet. Spread with pesto; sprinkle with cheese. Broil with tops 4 to 6 inches from heat 1 to 2 minutes or until edges of bread are golden brown.

3 Into 4 soup bowls, ladle soup. Top each serving with bread slice.

1 SERVING: Calories 260; Total Fat 7g (Saturated Fat 2g; Trans Fat 0g); Cholesterol 0mg; Sodium 910mg; Total Carbohydrate 39g (Dietary Fiber 4g); Protein 9g **EXCHANGES:** 1½ Starch, ½ Other Carbohydrate, 2 Vegetable, 1½ Fat **CARBOHYDRATE CHOICES:** 2½

make it a meal

This recipe is ideal for lunch or dinner. To complete the meal, add a simple tossed salad with a favorite dressing, and you're good to go.

meatless

grilled portabella and bell pepper sandwiches

PREP TIME **30 MINUTES**   START TO FINISH **30 MINUTES**   **6 SANDWICHES**

6 medium fresh portabella mushroom caps

1 large red bell pepper, cut into ¼-inch slices

1 large red onion, sliced

1 tablespoon olive or vegetable oil

½ teaspoon seasoned salt

1 round focaccia bread (8 or 9 inches)

¼ cup mayonnaise or salad dressing

¼ cup basil pesto

4 leaf lettuce leaves

1 Heat gas or charcoal grill. Brush mushrooms, bell pepper and onion with oil. Sprinkle with seasoned salt. Place vegetables in grill basket (grill "wok").

2 Place grill basket on grill. Cover grill; cook over medium heat 10 to 12 minutes, shaking grill basket occasionally to turn vegetables, until bell pepper and onion are crisp-tender and mushrooms are just tender.

3 Cut bread horizontally in half. In small bowl, mix mayonnaise and pesto; spread over cut sides of bread. Layer lettuce and grilled vegetables on bottom half of bread. Add top of bread. Cut into 6 wedges.

1 SANDWICH: Calories 350; Total Fat 22g (Saturated Fat 4.5g; Trans Fat 0g); Cholesterol 10mg; Sodium 470mg; Total Carbohydrate 28g (Dietary Fiber 2g); Protein 10g **EXCHANGES:** 1½ Starch, 1 Vegetable, ½ High-Fat Meat, 3½ Fat **CARBOHYDRATE CHOICES:** 2

instant success

It's easy to clean mushrooms just before using by wiping them off with a damp paper towel. If you find that the mushrooms are very watery after cooking, pat them dry before making the sandwiches.

meatless

fast veggie sides

Pick one or more of these tasty side dish ideas for your next meal—they're all easy and delicious!

1 Asparagus with Toasted Nuts and Citrus Zest: Top hot cooked asparagus spears with slivered almonds or pine nuts that have been toasted in melted butter in a skillet. Sprinkle with grated lemon or orange zest.

2 Broccoli Italian-Style: Toss hot cooked broccoli florets with warm zesty Italian dressing; sprinkle with grated Parmesan cheese or shredded Cheddar cheese.

3 Broccoli with Garlic and Herb Cream Cheese: Heat garlic and herb spreadable cheese in small saucepan over low heat, stirring frequently, until smooth and creamy. Spoon over cooked broccoli.

4 Cauliflower and Roasted Peppers: Toss hot cooked cauliflower florets with sliced roasted red bell peppers; sprinkle with basil and garlic powder.

5 Grape Tomato Toss: Cook and stir 1 cup whole grape tomatoes, 1 to 2 teaspoons jarred chopped garlic, ½ teaspoon dried Italian seasoning into 1 tablespoon olive oil just until heated. Add salt and pepper to taste.

6 Green Beans with Shaved Asiago: Drizzle cooked green beans with olive oil. Use vegetable peeler to shave pieces of Asiago or Parmesan cheese over the top.

7 Herbed Green Beans: Toss cooked green beans with garlic-pepper seasoning, chopped fresh basil and chopped fresh parsley.

8 Maple-Glazed Carrots: Stir 1 tablespoon each maple syrup and melted butter and toss with cooked baby carrots.

9 Sugar Snap Peas with Honey Butter: Stir 1 tablespoon each honey and melted butter and toss with cooked sugar snap peas. Sprinkle with honey-roasted peanuts.

10 *(no photo)* **Balsamic Beets:** Heat cooked beets, 1 tablespoon olive oil, 1 tablespoon balsamic vinegar, ¼ teaspoon salt and 1 to 2 tablespoons chopped fresh basil until heated and glazed.

11 *(no photo)* **Corn and Sun-Dried Tomatoes:** Toss cooked whole-kernel corn with sliced oil-packed sun-dried tomatoes. Sprinkle with basil or oregano and seasoned salt.

12 *(no photo)* **Garlic Summer Squash:** Cook 2 cloves chopped garlic in 1 tablespoon olive oil 1 to 2 minutes. Add 1 each medium zucchini and yellow summer squash, sliced. Cook 5 to 6 minutes, stirring frequently until tender. Add salt and pepper to taste.

side dishes

spicy stir-fried green beans

PREP TIME **20 MINUTES**   START TO FINISH **20 MINUTES**   6 SERVINGS (½ CUP EACH)

⅓   cup stir-fry sauce

2   teaspoons chili-garlic paste

2   tablespoons vegetable oil

6   cups fresh green beans, trimmed

1   teaspoon sesame seeds

1 In medium bowl, mix stir-fry sauce and chili-garlic paste; set aside.

2 In 12-inch nonstick skillet, heat oil over medium-high heat. Add green beans; toss in hot oil and cook 5 to 7 minutes, stirring every minute, until bright green and crisp-tender (mixture may spatter during cooking). Beans will sizzle, blister and brown in spots. Remove skillet from heat.

3 With slotted spoon, remove beans from skillet; add to sauce mixture in bowl. Toss to coat. Place in serving bowl; sprinkle with sesame seeds.

1 SERVING: Calories 100; Total Fat 5g (Saturated Fat 1g; Trans Fat 0g); Cholesterol 0mg; Sodium 470mg; Total Carbohydrate 11g (Dietary Fiber 4g); Protein 2g **EXCHANGES:** ½ Other Carbohydrate, 1 Vegetable, 1 Fat **CARBOHYDRATE CHOICES:** 1

instant success

For recipes like this that tend to spatter during cooking, use a spatter guard screen, available at many department and specialty food stores.

green beans with glazed shallots in lemon-dill butter

PREP TIME **15 MINUTES**   START TO FINISH **15 MINUTES**   **6 SERVINGS (ABOUT ½ CUP EACH)**

1 lb fresh green beans, trimmed
2 tablespoons butter
2 shallots, finely chopped
½ teaspoon sugar
1 teaspoon fresh lemon juice
1 tablespoon chopped fresh dill weed
¼ teaspoon salt

1 In 4-quart saucepan, heat 1 to 2 inches water to boiling. Add beans; boil uncovered 8 to 10 minutes or until crisp-tender. Drain; return to saucepan.

2 Meanwhile, in 10-inch skillet, melt butter over medium heat. Add shallots; cook 2 to 3 minutes, stirring occasionally, until crisp-tender. Stir in sugar. Cook 2 to 3 minutes longer, stirring occasionally, until shallots are glazed and brown. Stir in lemon juice, dill weed and salt.

3 Add shallot mixture to green beans; toss to coat.

1 SERVING: Calories 60; Total Fat 4g (Saturated Fat 2.5g; Trans Fat 0g); Cholesterol 10mg; Sodium 130mg; Total Carbohydrate 5g (Dietary Fiber 2g); Protein 1g **EXCHANGES:** 1 Vegetable, 1 Fat **CARBOHYDRATE CHOICES:** ½

instant success

Shallots look like mini onions and taste like a mild mix of garlic and onion. You can usually find them near the onions in the produce section of the supermarket.

side dishes

peas with mushrooms and thyme

PREP TIME **10 MINUTES**   START TO FINISH **10 MINUTES**   **6 SERVINGS**

1 tablespoon olive or vegetable oil
1 medium onion, diced (½ cup)
1 cup sliced fresh mushrooms
1 bag (16 oz) frozen sweet peas
¼ teaspoon coarse (kosher or sea) salt
⅛ teaspoon white pepper
1 teaspoon chopped fresh or ¼ teaspoon dried thyme leaves

1 In 10-inch skillet, heat oil over medium heat. Add onion and mushrooms; cook 3 minutes, stirring occasionally. Stir in peas. Cook 3 to 5 minutes, stirring occasionally, until vegetables are tender.

2 Sprinkle with salt, pepper and thyme. Serve immediately.

1 SERVING: Calories 80; Total Fat 2.5g (Saturated Fat 0g; Trans Fat 0g); Cholesterol 0mg; Sodium 150mg; Total Carbohydrate 11g (Dietary Fiber 3g); Protein 4g **EXCHANGES:** ½ Other Carbohydrate, 1 Vegetable, ½ Fat **CARBOHYDRATE CHOICES:** 1

easy add-on

Add a gourmet touch to this simple side dish by using an assortment of wild mushrooms like crimini, shiitake and portabellas.

asparagus and corn with honey-mustard glaze

PREP TIME **20 MINUTES**   START TO FINISH **20 MINUTES**   **5 SERVINGS (½ CUP EACH)**

1   **lb fresh asparagus spears**
1   **cup frozen whole-kernel corn**
2   **teaspoons Dijon mustard**
2   **teaspoons honey**
¼   **teaspoon lemon-pepper seasoning**

1 Snap off tough ends of asparagus spears. Cut spears into 1-inch pieces.

2 In 2-quart saucepan, heat ½ cup water to boiling. Add asparagus and corn; reduce heat. Simmer uncovered 5 to 8 minutes or until asparagus is crisp-tender; drain.

3 In small bowl, mix mustard, honey and lemon-pepper seasoning. Stir into hot vegetables.

1 SERVING: Calories 60; Total Fat 0g (Saturated Fat 0g; Trans Fat 0g); Cholesterol 0mg; Sodium 70mg; Total Carbohydrate 12g (Dietary Fiber 2g); Protein 3g **EXCHANGES:** ½ Other Carbohydrate, 1 Vegetable **CARBOHYDRATE CHOICES:** 1

instant success

Green beans, cut into 1-inch pieces, may be substituted for the asparagus.

side dishes

betty crocker quick & easy   277

cranberry-pistachio brussels sprouts

PREP TIME **25 MINUTES**   START TO FINISH **25 MINUTES**   **6 SERVINGS (ABOUT ½ CUP EACH)**

2   slices thick-sliced bacon

1   lb Brussels sprouts, trimmed and cut in half lengthwise

¼   cup chicken broth

⅓   cup sweetened dried cranberries

¼   cup roasted salted pistachio nuts

1   tablespoon honey

¼   teaspoon cracked black pepper

1 In 10-inch skillet, cook bacon over medium heat until crisp. Drain bacon on paper towels. Drain all but 1 tablespoon drippings from skillet.

2 Cook Brussels sprouts in drippings 3 to 4 minutes, stirring frequently, until just beginning to brown. Add broth; cover and reduce heat to medium-low. Cook 5 to 6 minutes longer or until broth evaporates and Brussels sprouts are tender. Crumble bacon; add to Brussels sprouts along with remaining ingredients. Toss to coat.

1 SERVING: Calories 110; Total Fat 4.5g (Saturated Fat 1g; Trans Fat 0g); Cholesterol 0mg; Sodium 170mg; Total Carbohydrate 14g (Dietary Fiber 2g); Protein 4g **EXCHANGES:** ½ Starch, 1 Vegetable, 1 Fat **CARBOHYDRATE CHOICES:** 1

instant success

Remove any discolored leaves from the Brussels sprouts. To keep the little beauties from falling apart while cooking, cut off only a thin slice from the stem end.

asian-style butternut squash

PREP TIME **15 MINUTES**   START TO FINISH **25 MINUTES**   **6 SERVINGS** (½ CUP EACH)

¼ cup water

1 small butternut squash, peeled, seeded and cut into ½-inch pieces (about 4 cups)

3 tablespoons packed brown sugar

2 tablespoons soy sauce

1½ teaspoons chili oil

¼ cup chopped green onions (4 medium)

1 In 10-inch nonstick skillet, heat water to boiling. Add squash; reduce heat to medium. Cover and simmer 7 to 10 minutes or until squash is almost tender when pierced with a fork.

2 Meanwhile, in small bowl, mix brown sugar, soy sauce, and chili oil.

3 Stir soy sauce mixture into squash and water in skillet. Heat to boiling; reduce heat to medium-low. Cook uncovered 2 minutes, stirring occasionally. Stir in onion; cook 2 minutes longer, stirring frequently, until squash is tender.

1 SERVING: Calories 80; Total Fat 1g (Saturated Fat 0g; Trans Fat 0g); Cholesterol 0mg; Sodium 310mg; Total Carbohydrate 16g (Dietary Fiber 1g); Protein 1g **EXCHANGES:** 1 Other Carbohydrate, ½ Vegetable **CARBOHYDRATE CHOICES:** 1

instant success

Chili oil is vegetable oil that has been infused with hot peppers. Characteristically red in color, it adds spicy heat to Asian dishes. Look for it near other Asian products at your supermarket. Once opened, it can be stored for up to 6 months at room temperature, or longer if refrigerated.

side dishes

edamame-corn toss

PREP TIME **25 MINUTES**   START TO FINISH **25 MINUTES**   **7 SERVINGS (½ CUP EACH)**

2   slices thick-sliced bacon,
    cut crosswise in half

½   cup chopped red bell pepper

1½ cups frozen shelled edamame
    (green) soybeans, thawed
    (from 12-oz bag)

2½ cups frozen whole-kernel corn,
    thawed

½   cup half-and-half

2   tablespoons chopped fresh
    oregano leaves

¼   teaspoon salt

¼   teaspoon black pepper

1 In 2-quart saucepan, cook bacon over medium-high heat until crisp. Drain bacon on paper towels. Drain all but 1 tablespoon drippings from saucepan. Reduce heat to medium; cook bell pepper in drippings 2 to 3 minutes, stirring occasionally, until tender.

2 Add edamame and corn; cook 3 minutes, stirring occasionally. Stir in half-and-half, oregano, salt and pepper. Cover and cook 5 to 6 minutes longer, stirring occasionally, until vegetables are tender. Crumble bacon; stir in into vegetable mixture.

1 SERVING: Calories 140; Total Fat 6g (Saturated Fat 2g; Trans Fat 0g); Cholesterol 10mg; Sodium 170mg; Total Carbohydrate 16g (Dietary Fiber 3g); Protein 7g **EXCHANGES:** ½ Starch, 1 Vegetable, ½ Very Lean Meat, 1 Fat **CARBOHYDRATE CHOICES:** 1

speed it up

To slash prep time for this recipe, start with precooked bacon. Microwave bacon as directed on package; crumble. Spray skillet with cooking spray to cook the bell pepper, then continue as directed.

side dishes

gingered baby carrots

PREP TIME **20 MINUTES**   START TO FINISH **20 MINUTES**   6 SERVINGS (½ CUP EACH)

1 bag (16 oz) ready-to-eat
   baby-cut carrots

¼ cup chopped pecans

3 tablespoons packed
   brown sugar

⅛ teaspoon ground cinnamon

1 tablespoon butter

1 tablespoon honey

1 tablespoon minced gingerroot

1 In 1-quart microwavable casserole, place carrots and 2 tablespoons water; cover with plastic wrap. Microwave on High 7 to 10 minutes until crisp-tender. Let stand covered 5 minutes. Drain; set aside.

2 Meanwhile, in 8-inch skillet, cook pecans, 1 tablespoon of the brown sugar and the cinnamon over medium heat about 3 minutes, stirring frequently, until pecans are toasted and glazed. Transfer from skillet to small bowl.

3 In same skillet, cook remaining 2 tablespoons brown sugar, the butter, honey and gingerroot over medium heat, stirring constantly, until bubbly. Add cooked carrots; cook 2 to 3 minutes longer, stirring frequently, until carrots are glazed and hot; sprinkle with pecans.

1 SERVING: Calories 160; Total Fat 9g (Saturated Fat 2g; Trans Fat 0g); Cholesterol 5mg; Sodium 70mg; Total Carbohydrate 18g (Dietary Fiber 3g); Protein 1g **EXCHANGES:** 1 Other Carbohydrate, 1 Vegetable, 2 Fat **CARBOHYDRATE CHOICES:** 1

speed it up

To quickly and easily remove the peel from fresh gingerroot, scrape the tip of a spoon over the peel.

side dishes

broccoli and squash medley

PREP TIME **30 MINUTES**   START TO FINISH **30 MINUTES**   **14 SERVINGS (½ CUP EACH)**

2 **bags (12 oz each) frozen cut broccoli**

2 **cups cubed (½ inch) peeled butternut squash (1½ lb)**

½ **cup fresh orange juice**

¼ **cup butter, melted**

½ **cup sweetened dried cranberries**

½ **cup finely chopped pecans, toasted**

1 **tablespoon grated orange zest**

1 **teaspoon salt**

1 Cook and drain broccoli as directed on bag. Meanwhile, in 12-inch skillet, cook squash in orange juice over medium-low heat 8 to 10 minutes, stirring frequently, until tender but firm.

2 Stir in butter, broccoli, cranberries, pecans, orange zest and salt; toss to coat. Serve immediately.

1 SERVING: Calories 110; Total Fat 6g (Saturated Fat 2.5g; Trans Fat 0g); Cholesterol 10mg; Sodium 210mg; Total Carbohydrate 12g (Dietary Fiber 2g); Protein 2g **EXCHANGES:** 1 Starch, 1 Fat **CARBOHYDRATE CHOICES:** 1

instant success

To toast the pecans, sprinkle in an ungreased skillet. Cook over medium heat 5 to 7 minutes, stirring frequently until pecans begin to brown, then stirring constantly until light brown.

lemon-spinach couscous

PREP TIME **15 MINUTES**   START TO FINISH **20 MINUTES**   6 SERVINGS (⅔ CUP EACH)

2 teaspoons olive oil
½ cup chopped red bell pepper
2 cloves garlic, finely chopped
1⅓ cups water
½ teaspoon salt
⅛ teaspoon black pepper
1 cup whole wheat couscous
2 teaspoons finely grated lemon zest
2 cups firmly packed fresh baby spinach leaves (3 oz)
   Lemon wedges, if desired

1 In 2-quart saucepan, heat oil over medium heat. Add bell pepper and garlic; cook 3 to 4 minutes, stirring frequently, until tender.

2 Stir in water, salt and pepper. Heat to boiling. Remove from heat; stir in couscous and lemon zest. Layer spinach on top of couscous. Cover; let stand about 5 minutes or until liquid is absorbed. With fork, stir spinach into couscous until spinach is wilted, about 1 minute. Serve with lemon wedges.

1 SERVING: Calories 140; Total Fat 2g (Saturated Fat 0g; Trans Fat 0g); Cholesterol 0mg; Sodium 210mg; Total Carbohydrate 25g (Dietary Fiber 3g); Protein 4g **EXCHANGES:** 1 Starch, ½ Other Carbohydrate, ½ Fat **CARBOHYDRATE CHOICES:** 1½

instant success

Couscous is a quick-cooking whole-grain pasta originating from the Mediterranean region. At the market, look for it near the other pasta or with the rice.

side dishes

curried veggie brown rice

PREP TIME **15 MINUTES**   START TO FINISH **15 MINUTES**   **8 SERVINGS (½ CUP EACH)**

2	cups chicken broth
1½	teaspoons curry powder
½	teaspoon salt
2	cups instant brown rice
1½	cups frozen mixed vegetables (from 12-oz bag)
⅓	cup raisins
2	tablespoons chopped fresh parsley

1 In 2-quart saucepan, heat broth, curry powder and salt to boiling. Stir in rice; reduce heat to medium-low. Cover and cook 3 minutes.

2 Add vegetables; cover and cook 4 to 6 minutes longer or until rice and vegetables are tender. Remove from heat; let stand 3 to 4 minutes or until liquid is absorbed; fluff with a fork. Stir in raisins and parsley.

1 SERVING: Calories 230; Total Fat 2g (Saturated Fat 0g; Trans Fat 0g); Cholesterol 0mg; Sodium 430mg; Total Carbohydrate 47g (Dietary Fiber 6g); Protein 6g **EXCHANGES:** 2 Starch, 1 Other Carbohydrate, ½ Vegetable **CARBOHYDRATE CHOICES:** 3

easy add-on

This flavor-packed side dish is a welcome addition to plain grilled chicken or pork. When topped with a dollop of chutney, it's like icing on the cake!

side dishes

cheesy vegetable risotto

PREP TIME **30 MINUTES**   START TO FINISH **30 MINUTES**   **8 SERVINGS (½ CUP EACH)**

1 tablespoon butter

2 tablespoons olive or vegetable oil

1 large onion, chopped (1 cup)

1 clove garlic, finely chopped

1 cup short-grain Arborio rice

1 carton (32 oz) reduced-sodium chicken broth (4 cups), warmed

1 bag (12 oz) frozen broccoli, carrots, cauliflower and cheese sauce

½ cup shredded Parmesan cheese (2 oz)

2 tablespoons chopped fresh parsley

¼ teaspoon coarse ground black pepper

1 In 10-inch nonstick skillet, heat butter and oil over medium-high heat until butter is melted. Cook onion and garlic in butter mixture 3 to 4 minutes, stirring frequently, until onion is tender.

2 Stir in rice. Cook, stirring occasionally, until edges of kernels are translucent. Stir in ½ cup of the broth. Cook and stir 2 to 3 minutes, until broth is absorbed.

3 Reduce heat to medium. Stir in 1½ cups of the broth; cook uncovered about 5 minutes, stirring frequently, until broth is absorbed. Stir in another 1 cup of the broth; cook uncovered about 5 minutes longer, stirring frequently, until broth is absorbed.

4 Stir in remaining 1 cup broth. Cook about 8 minutes, stirring frequently, until rice is tender and mixture is creamy.

5 Meanwhile, cook frozen vegetables as directed on bag. Stir vegetables, Parmesan cheese, parsley and pepper into rice mixture.

1 SERVING: Calories 200; Total Fat 7g (Saturated Fat 2.5g; Trans Fat 0g); Cholesterol 10mg; Sodium 840mg; Total Carbohydrate 26g (Dietary Fiber 1g); Protein 7g **EXCHANGES:** 1½ Starch, 1 Vegetable, 1 Fat **CARBOHYDRATE CHOICES:** 2

instant success

No fresh parsley? Toss in 2 teaspoons of dried parsley flakes or basil leaves. This delicious risotto is an ideal accompaniment to Herb-Seasoned Red Snapper (page 196) or Crispy Italian Bread Crumb–Coated Pork Chops (page 145).

orzo and spinach tabbouleh

PREP TIME **25 MINUTES**   START TO FINISH **25 MINUTES**   **12 SERVINGS (½ CUP EACH)**

1½   **cups orzo or rosamarina pasta (12 oz)**

3   **tablespoons olive oil**

3   **tablespoons fresh lemon juice**

1   **teaspoon chopped garlic**

½   **teaspoon salt**

2   **cups chopped English (seedless) cucumber**

1   **cup chopped fresh spinach**

½   **cup chopped fresh mint leaves**

1   **package (3 oz) dry-pack sun-dried tomatoes, chopped**

1 Cook and drain pasta as directed on package.

2 Meanwhile, in small bowl, mix oil, lemon juice, garlic and salt with whisk until blended. In medium bowl, combine cucumber, spinach, mint and tomatoes; add cooked pasta to spinach mixture. Pour dressing over salad; toss to coat. Serve immediately or cover and refrigerate for up to 1 hour.

1 SERVING: Calories 130; Total Fat 4g (Saturated Fat 0.5g; Trans Fat 0g); Cholesterol 0mg; Sodium 310mg; Total Carbohydrate 19g (Dietary Fiber 2g); Protein 4g **EXCHANGES:** 1 Starch, ½ Vegetable, ½ Fat **CARBOHYDRATE CHOICES:** 1

easy add-on

Add some crunch to this yummy salad by topping with toasted pine nuts. To toast pine nuts, sprinkle in an ungreased heavy skillet. Cook over medium heat 5 to 7 minutes, stirring frequently until nuts begin to brown, then stirring constantly until nuts are light golden brown.

cherry-pecan quinoa

PREP TIME **5 MINUTES**   START TO FINISH **20 MINUTES**   8 SERVINGS (½ CUP EACH)

- 2 cups water
- 1 cup quinoa, rinsed, well drained
- ½ teaspoon salt
- ½ teaspoon coarsely ground black pepper
- ½ cup chopped pecans
- ½ cup dried cherries, coarsely chopped
- ¼ cup finely chopped fresh cilantro or basil leaves
- 1 tablespoon grated orange zest

1 In 2-quart saucepan, heat water, quinoa, salt and pepper to boiling; reduce heat. Cover and simmer 12 to 15 minutes or until quinoa is tender and water is absorbed.

2 Stir in remaining ingredients. Serve warm.

1 SERVING: Calories 160; Total Fat 6g (Saturated Fat 0.5g; Trans Fat 0g); Cholesterol 0mg; Sodium 150mg; Total Carbohydrate 23g (Dietary Fiber 2g); Protein 4g **EXCHANGES:** 1 Starch, ½ Other Carbohydrate, 1 Fat **CARBOHYDRATE CHOICES:** 1½

easy add-on

Turn this side dish into a main dish by stirring in shredded rotisserie chicken. For extra flavor, add crumbled feta cheese.

side dishes

herbed confetti hash browns

PREP TIME **25 MINUTES**   START TO FINISH **25 MINUTES**   **4 SERVINGS (½ CUP EACH)**

2 **tablespoons olive oil**

2 **cups refrigerated diced potatoes with onion (from 1-lb 4-oz bag)**

1 **medium carrot, chopped**

1 **medium zucchini, chopped**

1 **teaspoon chopped fresh rosemary leaves**

1 **teaspoon chopped fresh thyme leaves**

¾ **teaspoon salt**

½ **teaspoon garlic powder**

1 In 12-inch nonstick skillet, heat oil over medium heat. Add all remaining ingredients; stir to mix.

2 Cook 15 to 20 minutes, stirring occasionally, until potatoes are golden brown and vegetables are tender.

1 SERVING: Calories 140; Total Fat 7g (Saturated Fat 1g; Trans Fat 0g); Cholesterol 0mg; Sodium 590mg; Total Carbohydrate 17g (Dietary Fiber 2g); Protein 2g **EXCHANGES:** 1 Other Carbohydrate, 1 Vegetable, 1½ Fat **CARBOHYDRATE CHOICES:** 1

easy add-on

If you like, serve these seasoned potatoes with a dollop of sour cream.

side dishes

smashed mexican potatoes

PREP TIME **5 MINUTES**   START TO FINISH **25 MINUTES**   **6 SERVINGS** (½ CUP EACH)

1   **lb small red potatoes,
     cut into 1-inch pieces**

½   **cup black beans, rinsed,
     drained (from 15-oz can)**

½   **cup frozen whole-kernel corn**

½   **cup shredded Colby–Monterey
     Jack cheese blend (2 oz)**

2   **tablespoons chopped fresh
     cilantro**

½   **teaspoon ground cumin**

½   **teaspoon salt**

1   **to 2 tablespoons milk**

1 In 2-quart saucepan, place potatoes; add enough water to cover potatoes. Heat to boiling; reduce heat. Cover and simmer 14 to 18 minutes or until potatoes are tender when pierced with a fork; drain. Return potatoes to saucepan; shake saucepan gently over low heat 1 to 2 minutes to evaporate any excess moisture; remove from heat. Mash potatoes with fork or potato masher, leaving some potato pieces in chunks.

2 In small microwavable bowl, combine beans and corn. Cover with plastic wrap; microwave on High 2 to 3 minutes or until hot.

3 Gently fold bean mixture, cheese, cilantro, cumin and salt into potatoes. Stir in milk, 1 tablespoon at a time, until desired consistency.

1 SERVING: Calories 130; Total Fat 3.5g (Saturated Fat 2g; Trans Fat 0g); Cholesterol 10mg; Sodium 310mg; Total Carbohydrate 20g (Dietary Fiber 3g); Protein 5g **EXCHANGES:** 1 Starch, ½ Vegetable, ½ Fat **CARBOHYDRATE CHOICES:** 1

easy add-on

For even more Mexican flavor, top potatoes with sliced avocado and a dollop of sour cream.

side dishes

california blt tossed salad

PREP TIME **15 MINUTES**   START TO FINISH **15 MINUTES**   **4 SERVINGS**

⅓ cup ranch dressing

½ teaspoon grated lemon zest

12 slices packaged precooked bacon (from 2.1-oz package)

1 bag (10 oz) American blend salad greens (iceberg lettuce, romaine, red cabbage, carrots and radishes)

1 large tomato, cut into wedges

1 avocado, pitted, peeled and cut into wedges

1 In small bowl, mix ranch dressing and lemon zest. Heat bacon as directed on package; cut into pieces.

2 In serving bowl, toss salad greens and bacon with dressing until coated. Garnish with tomato and avocado.

1 SERVING: Calories 280; Total Fat 23g (Saturated Fat 5g; Trans Fat 0g); Cholesterol 30mg; Sodium 510mg; Total Carbohydrate 8g (Dietary Fiber 4g); Protein 10g **EXCHANGES:** 2 Vegetable, 1 Lean Meat, 4 Fat **CARBOHYDRATE CHOICES:** ½

speed it up

Look for packages of precooked bacon near the regular bacon in the supermarket. It just needs to be reheated in the microwave.

20 minutes or less

cauliflower salad

PREP TIME **20 MINUTES**   START TO FINISH **20 MINUTES**   **16 SERVINGS (½ CUP EACH)**

- 10 slices bacon, cut into ½-inch pieces
- 1 cup mayonnaise or salad dressing
- ¼ cup sugar
- 1 medium head cauliflower (about 2 lb), separated into florets
- 1 small onion, finely chopped
- 1 small green bell pepper, finely chopped
- 8 oz Colby–Monterey Jack cheese blend, cut into ½-inch cubes

1 In 12-inch nonstick skillet over medium heat, cook bacon pieces 5 to 7 minutes or until crisp. Drain on paper towels; set aside.

2 In large bowl, stir together mayonnaise and sugar. Stir in cauliflower, onion and bell pepper until vegetables are coated with mayonnaise mixture.

3 Just before serving, stir in cheese. Sprinkle with bacon.

1 SERVING: Calories 210; Total Fat 17g (Saturated Fat 5g; Trans Fat 0g); Cholesterol 25mg; Sodium 280mg; Total Carbohydrate 6g (Dietary Fiber 1g); Protein 6g **EXCHANGES:** 1½ Vegetable, ½ High-Fat Meat, 2½ Fat **CARBOHYDRATE CHOICES:** ½

Recipe courtesy of Shreya Sasaki, RecipeMatcher, recipematcher.com

instant success

It's okay to vary this recipe to your taste. Low-fat mayonnaise, turkey bacon and green or yellow bell pepper are all good substitutions.

side dishes

black bean–chili salad

PREP TIME **15 MINUTES**   START TO FINISH **15 MINUTES**   **4 SERVINGS**

DRESSING

- ¼ **cup red wine vinegar**
- 2 **tablespoons vegetable oil**
- ½ **teaspoon chili powder**
- ¼ **teaspoon ground cumin**
- 1 **small clove garlic,
  finely chopped**

SALAD

- 1 **cup frozen whole-kernel corn,
  cooked, drained**
- 1 **cup finely chopped peeled
  jicama**
- 1 **medium tomato, seeded,
  chopped (¾ cup)**
- 2 **medium green onions, sliced
  (2 tablespoons)**
- 2 **cans (15 oz each) black beans,
  rinsed, drained**

1 In large glass or plastic bowl, mix dressing ingredients.

2 Stir salad ingredients into dressing until well mixed.

1 SERVING: Calories 290; Total Fat 8g (Saturated Fat 1g; Trans Fat 0g); Cholesterol 0mg; Sodium 710mg; Total Carbohydrate 42g (Dietary Fiber 12g); Protein 12g **EXCHANGES:** 2½ Starch, ½ Vegetable, ½ Lean Meat, 1 Fat **CARBOHYDRATE CHOICES:** 3

instant success

What's jicama? Sometimes referred to as the "Mexican potato," this sweet and nutty root vegetable can be enjoyed raw or cooked. Look for it in the produce section of the store.

20 minutes or less

lo mein noodle salad

PREP TIME **20 MINUTES**   START TO FINISH **20 MINUTES**   **12 SERVINGS (½ CUP EACH)**

SALAD

- **1 package (8 oz) lo mein noodles**
- **1 bag (10 or 12 oz) frozen shelled edamame (green) soybeans**
- **1 large red bell pepper, chopped (1½ cups)**
- **4 medium green onions, sliced (¼ cup)**

DRESSING

- **⅓ cup rice vinegar**
- **⅓ cup peanut butter**
- **¼ cup soy sauce**
- **2 tablespoons packed brown sugar**
- **2 tablespoons vegetable oil**
- **¼ teaspoon crushed red pepper flakes**

1 Break lo mein noodles into thirds. Cook as directed on package. Rinse with cold water; drain.

2 Meanwhile, cook edamame as directed on bag; drain.

3 In medium bowl, toss noodles, edamame, bell pepper and onions.

4 In small bowl, beat dressing ingredients with whisk until well blended. Spoon over noodle mixture; toss to coat. Serve immediately, or cover and refrigerate until serving time.

1 SERVING: Calories 200; Total Fat 8g (Saturated Fat 1.5g; Trans Fat 0g); Cholesterol 0mg; Sodium 340mg; Total Carbohydrate 24g (Dietary Fiber 3g); Protein 8g **EXCHANGES:** 1½ Starch, ½ Lean Meat, 1 Fat **CARBOHYDRATE CHOICES:** 1½

easy add-on

Garnish the salad with 1 to 2 tablespoons chopped fresh cilantro leaves.

side dishes

mixed greens salad with warm walnut dressing

PREP TIME **15 MINUTES**   START TO FINISH **15 MINUTES**   **4 SERVINGS**

6 **cups mixed field greens (about 5 oz)**

6 **tablespoons olive or vegetable oil**

½ **cup walnut halves**

3 **tablespoons red wine vinegar**

¼ **teaspoon salt**

1 Among 4 salad plates, divide field greens.

2 In medium microwavable bowl, place 1 tablespoon of the oil. Add walnut halves; stir to coat. Microwave uncovered on High 2 minutes 30 seconds to 3 minutes, stirring every 30 seconds, until walnuts are fragrant.

3 Stir in remaining 5 tablespoons oil and the vinegar. Microwave uncovered on High about 30 seconds or until dressing is warm but not boiling. Add salt; stir until dressing is well mixed. Pour over salads. Serve immediately.

1 SERVING: Calories 280; Total Fat 28g (Saturated Fat 3.5g; Trans Fat 0g); Cholesterol 0mg; Sodium 160mg; Total Carbohydrate 3g (Dietary Fiber 1g); Protein 2g **EXCHANGES:** 1 Vegetable, 5½ Fat **CARBOHYDRATE CHOICES:** 0

instant success

For a gourmet flair, try using balsamic or raspberry-flavored vinegar.

20 minutes or less

mixed greens with fruit and raspberry dressing

PREP TIME **10 MINUTES**   START TO FINISH **10 MINUTES**   **4 SERVINGS**

2 **cups torn mixed salad greens**

1 **can (8 oz) pineapple tidbits, drained**

1 **cup fresh raspberries**

2 **medium bananas, sliced**

2 **medium green onions, sliced (2 tablespoons)**

½ **cup fat-free raspberry vinaigrette**

1 Among 4 salad plates, divide salad greens, pineapple, raspberries, bananas and green onions.

2 Drizzle each salad with 2 tablespoons vinaigrette. Serve immediately.

1 SERVING: Calories 150; Total Fat 0.5g (Saturated Fat 0g; Trans Fat 0g); Cholesterol 0mg; Sodium 250mg; Total Carbohydrate 35g (Dietary Fiber 5g); Protein 2g **EXCHANGES:** 1 Fruit, 1½ Other Carbohydrate **CARBOHYDRATE CHOICES:** 2

easy add-on

To make a main-dish salad, top with a grilled chicken breast or several strips of leftover roast beef. Also, you can mix and match fruits for the salad. Try blueberries instead of raspberries or cut-up fresh mango instead of the pineapple.

side dishes

beet and baby greens salad

PREP TIME **10 MINUTES**   START TO FINISH **20 MINUTES**   **4 SERVINGS**

4 small red or gold beets, stems removed, peeled and cut into ¼-inch slices (about 2 cups)

¼ cup olive oil

3 tablespoons balsamic vinegar

4 cups mixed baby greens (from 5-oz package)

½ cup chopped red onion

½ cup crumbled feta cheese (2 oz)

1 In 9-inch microwavable glass pie plate, place beets, overlapping slightly. Add ¼ cup water; cover with plastic wrap. Microwave on High 4 to 5 minutes or until almost tender when pierced with a fork; drain.

2 Meanwhile in small bowl, beat oil and vinegar with whisk until blended. Place baby greens on large serving plate; arrange cooked beets on baby greens. Drizzle dressing over beets and baby greens; top with onion and cheese.

1 SERVING: Calories 230; Total Fat 17g (Saturated Fat 4g; Trans Fat 0g); Cholesterol 15mg; Sodium 240mg; Total Carbohydrate 14g (Dietary Fiber 4g); Protein 4g **EXCHANGES:** ½ Other Carbohydrate, 1 Vegetable, ½ Medium-Fat Meat, 3 Fat **CARBOHYDRATE CHOICES:** 1

instant success

If your beets are large, cut them in half, then cut into ¼-inch slices. If using both red and gold beets, microwave them with the red on one side of the pie plate and the gold on the other, so just a little of the red color leaches onto the gold beets, or microwave red and gold beets separately. If the two colors are arranged randomly, the gold beets will all become red.

spring raspberry salad

PREP TIME **20 MINUTES**   START TO FINISH **20 MINUTES**   8 SERVINGS (1 CUP EACH)

¼ cup chopped walnuts

2 tablespoons sugar

1 bag (5 oz) torn mixed salad greens

2 cups fresh raspberries

½ small red onion, thinly sliced (½ cup)

½ cup chopped dates

⅓ cup balsamic vinaigrette dressing

½ cup crumbled goat cheese (2 oz)

1 In 8-inch nonstick skillet, cook walnuts and sugar over low heat about 10 minutes, stirring frequently, until sugar is melted and walnuts are coated. Cool; break apart.

2 In large bowl, combine salad greens, raspberries, onion and dates. Just before serving, pour dressing over salad; toss gently to coat. Top with cheese and sugared walnuts.

1 SERVING: Calories 160; Total Fat 8g (Saturated Fat 2g; Trans Fat 0g); Cholesterol 5mg; Sodium 150mg; Total Carbohydrate 19g (Dietary Fiber 4g); Protein 3g **EXCHANGES:** 1 Fruit, 1 Vegetable, ½ High-Fat Meat, ½ Fat **CARBOHYDRATE CHOICES:** 1

Recipe courtesy of Cheri Liefeld of Adventures in the Kitchen, adventuresinthekitchen.com

instant success

Walnuts keep well in the freezer, so it's easy to keep some on hand to make tasty recipes like this.

side dishes

apple-gorgonzola salad with red wine vinaigrette

PREP TIME **20 MINUTES**   START TO FINISH **20 MINUTES**   **6 SERVINGS**

VINAIGRETTE

- ⅓ **cup olive or vegetable oil**
- ¼ **cup red wine vinegar**
- 2 **tablespoons sugar**
- 1 **teaspoon Dijon mustard**
- 1 **clove garlic, finely chopped**

SALAD

- 1 **bag (10 oz) mixed baby greens or Italian-blend salad greens**
- 1 **medium red or green apple, chopped (1 cup)**
- ½ **cup crumbled Gorgonzola or blue cheese (2 oz)**
- ⅓ **cup chopped walnuts, toasted**

1 In small bowl, beat vinaigrette ingredients with whisk until smooth.

2 In large bowl, toss salad ingredients with vinaigrette just before serving.

1 SERVING: Calories 230; Total Fat 19g (Saturated Fat 4g; Trans Fat 0g); Cholesterol 5mg; Sodium 170mg; Total Carbohydrate 10g (Dietary Fiber 2g); Protein 4g **EXCHANGES:** ½ Other Carbohydrate, ½ High-Fat Meat, 3 Fat **CARBOHYDRATE CHOICES:** ½

instant success

To toast walnuts, sprinkle in an ungreased skillet. Cook over medium heat 5 to 7 minutes, stirring frequently until pecans begin to brown, then stirring constantly until light brown.

greek salad

PREP TIME **20 MINUTES**   START TO FINISH **20 MINUTES**   8 SERVINGS (ABOUT 1¾ CUPS EACH)

DRESSING

- ¼ cup olive oil
- 2 tablespoons fresh lemon juice
- ½ teaspoon sugar
- 1½ teaspoons Dijon mustard
- ¼ teaspoon salt
- ⅛ teaspoon black pepper

SALAD

- 5 cups fresh baby spinach
- 1 head Boston lettuce, torn into bite-size pieces (4 cups)
- 1 cup crumbled feta cheese (4 oz)
- 24 pitted kalamata or Greek olives
- 4 medium green onions, sliced (¼ cup)
- 3 medium tomatoes, cut into wedges
- 1 medium cucumber, sliced

1 In tightly covered container, shake all dressing ingredients.

2 In large bowl, toss salad ingredients and dressing. Serve immediately.

1 SERVING: Calories 140; Total Fat 11g (Saturated Fat 3.5g; Trans Fat 0g); Cholesterol 15mg; Sodium 680mg; Total Carbohydrate 6g (Dietary Fiber 2g); Protein 4g **EXCHANGES:** 1 Vegetable, 2½ Fat **CARBOHYDRATE CHOICES:** ½

instant success

Extra-large pitted ripe olives may be substituted for the kalamata olives. Also, you may use chopped red onion instead of the green onions.

side dishes

grilled summer squash medley

PREP TIME **30 MINUTES**   START TO FINISH **30 MINUTES**   **4 SERVINGS**

2 **small zucchini, cut into ¼-inch slices**

2 **small yellow summer squash, cut into ¼-inch slices**

6 **mini pattypan squash, cut in half**

¼ **cup citrus vinaigrette dressing**

2 **medium plum (Roma) tomatoes, sliced**

2 **tablespoons chopped fresh cilantro**

1 Heat gas or charcoal grill. In large bowl, toss zucchini, summer squash, pattypan squash and dressing. With slotted spoon, place squash in grill basket (grill "wok"). Reserve dressing in bowl.

2 Place grill basket on grill over medium heat. Cover grill; cook 10 to 13 minutes, shaking basket or stirring squash occasionally, until crisp-tender. Return squash to bowl with dressing. Add tomatoes and cilantro; toss to coat.

1 SERVING: Calories 100; Total Fat 4.5g (Saturated Fat 0g; Trans Fat 0g); Cholesterol 0mg; Sodium 270mg; Total Carbohydrate 12g (Dietary Fiber 4g); Protein 3g **EXCHANGES:** 2 Vegetable, 1 Fat **CARBOHYDRATE CHOICES:** 1

instant success

Look for the citrus vinaigrette dressing with the salad dressings and sauces. If it's not available, balsamic and Asian vinaigrettes work well in this recipe.

deliciously easy salad combos

1 Asparagus and Parmesan Salad: Snap off tough ends of asparagus. Place spears in boiling water in 10-inch skillet; boil 2 minutes. Place in cold water to chill. Arrange 5 or 6 spears on each serving plate; drizzle with olive oil and balsamic vinegar. Sprinkle with coarse salt, pepper and shaved or shredded Parmesan cheese.

2 Classic Wedge Salad: Cut medium head of iceberg lettuce into 4 to 6 wedges; place on individual serving plates. Top each with about 2 tablespoons blue cheese dressing and 2 tablespoons cooked bacon pieces.

3 Cranberry–Toasted Walnut Slaw: Make homemade creamy coleslaw (bag of coleslaw blend and coleslaw dressing) or pick it up at the deli. Stir in ¼ cup each dried cranberries and walnut pieces.

4 Cukes and Tomatoes: On serving platter or individual serving plates, arrange cucumber slices or chunks with tomato wedges or slices. Sprinkle with salt and pepper; drizzle with your favorite dressing or just a splash of balsamic vinegar.

5 Greens and Melon Salad: Arrange mixed greens on serving platter or individual serving plates. Top each salad with ½ cup cubed watermelon, cantaloupe and honeydew melon. Drizzle with Italian or vinaigrette dressing.

6 Hearts of Palm Vinaigrette: Drain canned or jarred hearts of palm; cut into ¼-inch-thick slices; drizzle with Caesar or Italian dressing; sprinkle with pepper.

7 Honey-Nut Pineapple Slaw: Make homemade creamy coleslaw (bag of coleslaw blend and coleslaw dressing) or pick it up at the deli. Stir in ½ cup canned pineapple tidbits and honey-roasted peanuts.

8 Mango, Avocado and Raspberry Salad: On serving platter or individual serving plates, arrange ripe avocado slices and mango slices. Drizzle with raspberry vinaigrette; sprinkle with slivered almonds and pepper.

greens for salads

Butterhead Lettuce
(Boston)

Mesclun

Mâche

Escarole

Collard Greens

Dandelion
Greens

Mustard
Greens

Spinach

Frisée

Beet
Greens

Watercress

Radicchio

Romaine
Lettuce

Arugula

Curly Endive

Iceberg
Lettuce

Leaf Lettuce
(Red and Green)

Belgian Endive

Chard

metric conversion guide

Volume

U.S. UNITS	CANADIAN METRIC	AUSTRALIAN METRIC
¼ teaspoon	1 mL	1 ml
½ teaspoon	2 mL	2 ml
1 teaspoon	5 mL	5 ml
1 tablespoon	15 mL	20 ml
¼ cup	50 mL	60 ml
⅓ cup	75 mL	80 ml
½ cup	125 mL	125 ml
⅔ cup	150 mL	170 ml
¾ cup	175 mL	190 ml
1 cup	250 mL	250 ml
1 quart	1 liter	1 liter
1½ quarts	1.5 liters	1.5 liters
2 quarts	2 liters	2 liters
2½ quarts	2.5 liters	2.5 liters
3 quarts	3 liters	3 liters
4 quarts	4 liters	4 liters

Weight

U.S. UNITS	CANADIAN METRIC	AUSTRALIAN METRIC
1 ounce	30 grams	30 grams
2 ounces	55 grams	60 grams
3 ounces	85 grams	90 grams
4 ounces (¼ pound)	115 grams	125 grams
8 ounces (½ pound)	225 grams	225 grams
16 ounces (1 pound)	455 grams	500 grams
1 pound	455 grams	0.5 kilogram

Measurements

INCHES	CENTIMETERS
1	2.5
2	5.0
3	7.5
4	10.0
5	12.5
6	15.0
7	17.5
8	20.5
9	23.0
10	25.5
11	28.0
12	30.5
13	33.0

Temperatures

FAHRENHEIT	CELSIUS
32°	0°
212°	100°
250°	120°
275°	140°
300°	150°
325°	160°
350°	180°
375°	190°
400°	200°
425°	220°
450°	230°
475°	240°
500°	260°

Note: The recipes in this cookbook have not been developed or tested using metric measures. When converting recipes to metric, some variations in quality may be noted.

index

Page numbers in *italics* indicated illustrations

recipe testing and calculating nutrition information

Recipe Testing:

- Large eggs and 2% milk were used unless otherwise indicated.
- Fat-free, low-fat, low-sodium or lite products were not used unless indicated.
- No nonstick cookware or bakeware was used unless otherwise indicated. No dark-colored, black or insulated bakeware was used.
- When a pan is specified, a metal pan was used; a baking dish or pie plate means ovenproof glass was used.
- An electric hand mixer was used for mixing only when mixer speeds are specified.

Calculating Nutrition:

- The first ingredient was used wherever a choice is given, such as 1/3 cup sour cream or plain yogurt.
- The first amount was used wherever a range is given, such as 3- to 3½-pound whole chicken.
- The first serving number was used wherever a range is given, such as 4 to 6 servings.
- "If desired" ingredients were not included.
- Only the amount of a marinade or frying oil that is absorbed was included.

q

Complete your cookbook library with these *Betty Crocker* titles

Betty Crocker 30-Minute Meals for Diabetes

Betty Crocker The 300 Calorie Cookbook

Betty Crocker Baking Basics

Betty Crocker Baking for Today

Betty Crocker's Best Bread Machine Cookbook

Betty Crocker's Best-Loved Recipes

Betty Crocker The Big Book of Cookies

Betty Crocker The Big Book of Cupcakes

Betty Crocker The Big Book of Slow Cooker, Casseroles & More

Betty Crocker The Big Book of Weeknight Dinners

Betty Crocker Bisquick® II Cookbook

Betty Crocker Bisquick® Impossibly Easy Pies

Betty Crocker Bisquick® to the Rescue

Betty Crocker Christmas Cookbook

Betty Crocker's Cook Book for Boys and Girls

Betty Crocker Cookbook, 11th Edition— *The* **BIG RED** *Cookbook*®

Betty Crocker Cookbook, Bridal Edition

Betty Crocker's Cooking Basics

Betty Crocker's Cooky Book, Facsimile Edition

Betty Crocker Country Cooking

Betty Crocker Decorating Cakes and Cupcakes

Betty Crocker's Diabetes Cookbook

Betty Crocker Easy Everyday Vegetarian

Betty Crocker's Easy Slow Cooker Dinners

Betty Crocker's Eat and Lose Weight

Betty Crocker Fix-with-a-Mix Desserts

Betty Crocker Gluten-Free Cooking

Betty Crocker Grilling Made Easy

Betty Crocker Healthy Heart Cookbook

Betty Crocker's Indian Home Cooking

Betty Crocker's Italian Cooking

Betty Crocker's Kids Cook!

Betty Crocker Living with Cancer Cookbook

Betty Crocker Low-Carb Lifestyle Cookbook

Betty Crocker's Low-Fat, Low-Cholesterol Cooking Today

Betty Crocker Money Saving Meals

Betty Crocker More Slow Cooker Recipes

Betty Crocker's New Cake Decorating

Betty Crocker One-Dish Meals

Betty Crocker's Picture Cook Book, Facsimile Edition

Betty Crocker's Slow Cooker Cookbook

Betty Crocker Ultimate Bisquick® Cookbook

Betty Crocker's Ultimate Cake Mix Cookbook

Betty Crocker Why It Works